THE SURPRISING WORK OF GOD

FRANCISCO LEE
Kyoung - Won

THE
SURPRISING
WORK OF
GOD

JONATHAN
EDWARDS

[w] *Whitaker House*

All Scripture quotations are from the *King James Version* (KJV) of the Bible.

THE SURPRISING WORK OF GOD

ISBN: 0-88368-237-0
Printed in the United States of America
Copyright © 1997 by Whitaker House

Whitaker House
30 Hunt Valley Circle
New Kensington, PA 15068

Library of Congress Cataloguing-in-Publication Data

Edwards, Jonathan, 1703–1758.
    The surprising work of God / by Jonathan Edwards.
        p.   cm.
    ISBN 0-88368-237-0 (trade paper)
      1. Great Awakening—Early works to 1800. 2. Revivals—New England—
Early works to 1800.   3. New England—Church history—Early works to 1800.
4. Edwards, Jonathan, 1703–1758.   5. Revivals—Massachusetts—
Northampton—Early works to 1800.   6. Northampton (Mass.)—Church
history—18th century—Early works to 1800. I. Title.
BR520.E55   1997
277'.407—dc21   97-30554

1 2 3 4 5 6 7 8 9 10 11 12 / 06 05 04 03 02 01 00 99 98 97

What follows is Jonathan Edwards' personal, eyewitness account of the awesome move of the Holy Spirit throughout New England during the Great Awakening, 1734–35.

Contents

Chapter 1

A General History of the Revival

When several distinguished pastors and congregations in this region became aware of the wonderful work of God in Northampton, Massachusetts, and surrounding towns, they asked me to inform them of it in greater detail. Being a pastor in Northampton, I am quite familiar with many cases in which God has worked through and among the people during this revival. I hope, through this book, that I can acquaint you with the details of this work, now called the Great Awakening. And so, in as just and faithful a manner as I may, I proceed to show you God's hand in this wonderful work.

THE TOWN OF NORTHAMPTON

I suppose the general population of Northampton is as temperate, orderly, and good as people in any part of New England. Yet, I believe they have been preserved from error and a variety of sects and opinions more than individuals in other areas. The fact that Northampton is so far inland, at a distance from seaports and in a corner of the country, has doubtless been one reason why we have not been corrupted with vice to the degree that most other areas have been. But, without question, the religion and good order of the area and its purity in doctrine have, under God, been very much due to the great abilities and the eminent piety of my honored grandfather, Rev. Stoddard.

I suppose that, of all the communities in New England, we have been the freest from unhappy divisions and quarrels in our ecclesiastical and religious affairs until the recent and lamentable Springfield contention. This contention consists of heated debates among both the pastors and the people, on account of differing opinions about the principles of a certain minister, Robert Breck. There has been much arguing over the steps taken to procure this particular minister's ordination.

Because Northampton is separated from other parts of the province and has comparatively little connection with them, we have always managed our ecclesiastical affairs within ourselves. It is the way in which the county, from its infancy, has gone on, by the practical agreement of all. This is the way in which our peace and good order have been maintained.

The town of Northampton is about eighty-two years old, and now in 1736 it has about two hundred families, which tend to dwell more compactly together than any town of such a size in this part of the country. This probably has been the reason why both our corruptions and reformations have been, from time to time, the more swiftly propagated from one person to another through the town. The town in general, so far as I can judge, is comprised of rational and intelligent people. Many of them have been noted for religion and for their distinct knowledge in things that relate to heart religion and Christian experience.

MINISTERS IN THE TOWN

I am the third minister who has settled in the town. The Rev. Eleazer Mather, who was the first, was ordained in July 1669. He was one whose heart was very much in his work, and his labors for the good of precious souls were abundant. He had a high esteem and great love for his people and was blessed with great success. My grandfather, the Rev. Stoddard, who succeeded him, first came to the town the November after Rev. Mather's death. However, Rev. Stoddard was not ordained until September 11, 1672, and he died February 11, c. 1729. He continued in the work of the ministry here for nearly sixty years.

As Rev. Stoddard was eminent and renowned for his gifts and grace, so he was blessed from the beginning with extraordinary success in his ministry. Many souls were converted under his pastorship. He had five harvests, as he called them. The first was about fifty-seven years ago, the second about fifty-three, the third about forty, the fourth about twenty-four, the fifth and last about eighteen years ago. Some of these times were much more remarkable than others, and the ingathering of souls more plentiful. The harvests of about fifty-three, forty, and twenty-four years ago were much greater than either the first or the last. Nonetheless, in each of them, I have heard my grandfather say, the greater part of the young people in the town seemed to be the ones concerned about their eternal salvation.

DEGENERATION AND DULLNESS

After the last of these harvests, there came a far more degenerate time (at least among the young people) than ever before. Rev. Stoddard had the comfort, before he died, of seeing a time of divine work among some, and a considerable ingathering of souls. This occurred even after I was settled with him in the ministry, which was about two years before his death. And I have reason to bless God for the great advantage I received from it. In those two years, there were nearly twenty people who were converted under Rev. Stoddard, but there was no general awakening of any kind. At that time, the greater part of the people seemed to be very insensible of the things of religion and engaged in other cares and pursuits.

Just after my grandfather's death, it seemed to be a time of extraordinary dullness in religion. Licentiousness prevailed among the youth of the town; many of them were very much addicted to walking the streets at night with evil intentions, to frequenting the taverns, and to lewd practices. Some, by their example, exceedingly corrupted others. It was frequently their manner to get together for mirth and frivolity in meetings of both sexes, which they called *frolics;* and they would often spend the greater part of the night in them, without regard to any order in the families they belonged to. Indeed, family government did fail in the town during that time.

It became customary with many of our young people to conduct themselves indecently in church services, a practice that doubtless would not have prevailed to such a degree if my grandfather had been able to observe them as he once had. Through his great age (though he retained his powers surprisingly to the last), he was not able to watch over them so carefully.

There had also long prevailed in the town a spirit of contention between two parties, which had for many years been divided. Their division allowed them to maintain a jealousy toward one another, and they were prepared to oppose one another in all public affairs.

YOUNG PEOPLE ARE CHANGED

Yet, in two or three years after Rev. Stoddard's death, there began to be an obvious amendment to these evils. The young people showed more of a disposition to listen to counsel, and little by little they abandoned their silly meetings. Their conduct at the public worship grew observably more decent, and there were more who manifested a religious concern than there used to be.

Near the end of the year 1733, the young people here began to show a very unusual flexibility and yielding to advice. For a long time it had been their habit to make Monday evenings, after our public lecture, to be the times of their mirth and company-keeping. Although it had never been our custom to observe Monday evenings as part of the holy time, but rather Saturday evenings, a sermon was now preached concerning the evil tendency of the youths' practice. They were urged to reform it, and parents were urged to govern their families with more care and to keep their children at home during these times.

The heads of families were also urged to meet together the next day, in their various neighborhoods, to understand each other's minds. This was done accordingly, and the idea was complied with throughout the town. However, parents found little or no reason to exercise authority over their children in this case. The young people were already convinced by what they had heard from the pulpit and were willing to comply with the counsel that had been given. The preacher's advice was immediately and, I suppose, almost universally complied with. As a result, there was a thorough reformation of these disorders at that time, which has continued ever since.

RELIGIOUS CONCERN SPREADS

Almost immediately after this, there began to appear a remarkable religious concern in a little village called Pascommuck, where a few families were settled at about three miles from the main part of the town. At this place, a number of people seemed to be under the saving influence of the Holy Spirit. In April 1734, a young man there, in the bloom of his youth, died a very sudden and awful death. He had been violently seized with pleurisy and had immediately become very delirious. He died in about two days, which (along with what was preached publicly on that occasion) much affected many young people.

This was followed by the death of a young married woman, who, before she was ill, had been considerably troubled in mind about the salvation of her soul. She was in great distress in the beginning of her illness, but seemed to have satisfying evidences of God's mercy to her before her death. She died very full of comfort, in a most earnest and moving manner warning and counseling others. This seemed to contribute to sobering the spirits of many young people in the town, and more of a religious concern began to evidently appear on people's minds.

In the fall of that year, I strongly urged the young people that they should agree among themselves to spend the evenings after lectures in social religion. To that end, I suggested that they divide themselves into several companies to meet in various parts of the town. This was accordingly done, and those meetings have been continued ever since, and the example imitated by older people. This was followed by the death of an elderly person, which was accompanied by many unusual circumstances, by which many were much moved and affected.

THE CONTROVERSY OVER ARMINIANISM

Around this time, a great noise began in this part of the country about Arminianism, which seemed to threaten the interest of religion here. Arminianism opposes the absolute predestination in which Calvin believed. Those who practiced vital piety trembled in fear of the result of the controversy over this matter; but it seemed, contrary to their fear, that Arminianism was strongly overruled by the promoting of religion. Many who considered themselves to be in a Christless condition seemed to be awakened by the controversy, with fear that God was about to withdraw from the land and that we would be given up to unorthodox and corrupt principles, and that then their opportunity for obtaining salvation would be past.

Many who began to doubt some of the truth of the doctrines they had been taught beforehand, seemed to have a kind of trembling fear along with their doubts, lest they should be led into obscure paths to their eternal ruin. And, with much concern and fixedness of mind, they seemed eager to find out what was necessary for them to be accepted by God. On that occasion, there were some things said publicly concerning justification by faith alone.

Although it was considered a great fault for the pulpit to be found meddling with the controversy at that time—and though it was ridiculed by many elsewhere—it proved to be a word spoken in season here. A very remarkable blessing came from heaven to the people in Northampton because of it. They received from the pulpit a satisfying answer to the main thing in question, about which they had much doubt and concern. And now their minds were engaged even more earnestly to seek acceptance with God and to be saved in the way of the Gospel, for they had come to see the Gospel as the true and only way.

Chapter 2

The Spirit Moves among the People

In the latter part of December 1734, the Spirit of God began to set in extraordinarily and to work wonderfully among us. Very suddenly, one after another, five or six people were miraculously converted, as far as anyone could tell. I was particularly surprised by the story of a young woman who had been one of the greatest company-keepers in the whole town. When she came to speak with me, I had never heard that she was serious about anything. Yet, by the conversation I then had with her, it appeared to me that what she gave an account of was a glorious work of God's infinite power and sovereign grace.

She told me that God had given her a new heart, truly broken and sanctified. I could not then doubt it, and I have seen much in my acquaintance with her since to confirm it. Though the work in this woman's life was glorious, I was filled with concern about the effect it might have upon others. I was ready to conclude (though too rashly) that some people would be hardened by it in carelessness and looseness of life, and that they would use it as a reason to open their mouths in reproach of religion. However, the event was the reverse, to a wonderful degree. God made it, more than anything else that ever came to pass in the town, the greatest occasion of awakening to others.

Through my private conversations with many of the people, I have had abundant opportunity to know the effect this woman's story had upon them. The news of it seemed to be almost like a flash of lightning upon the hearts of young people all over the town, and upon many others. Those people among us who used to be farthest from seriousness, and who I most feared would make an ill improvement of her story, seemed to be awakened by it. Many went to talk with the young woman concerning what she had met with; and what had come about in her seemed to be to the satisfaction of everyone who did so.

RELIGION AFFECTS DAILY LIFE

Soon after this, a great and earnest concern about the things of religion and the eternal world became universal in all parts of the town, among people of all social positions and all ages. The noise among the dry bones became louder and louder. (See Ezekiel 37:1–7.) Talk about anything besides spiritual and eternal things was soon thrown by the wayside. All the conversation, in all companies and upon all occasions, was only about religious matters, unless it was necessary for people to discuss other matters in carrying on their ordinary secular business. Discourse on anything besides religion would scarcely be tolerated in any gathering. The minds of the people were wonderfully removed from the cares of the world.

The people seemed to follow their worldly business more as a part of their duty than from any attachment they had to it. It now seemed that the temptation was to neglect worldly affairs too much and to spend too much time in the immediate exercise of religion. This was highly misrepresented by reports that were spread into other regions, as though the people here had completely thrown aside all worldly business and had committed themselves entirely to reading and praying and such religious exercises.

Although people did not ordinarily neglect their worldly business, religion was the great concern among all sorts of people. The world was simply incidental to them. The only thing on their minds was to obtain the kingdom of heaven, and everyone appeared to be pressing into it. The fixedness of their hearts in this great concern could not be hidden; it appeared on their faces. It then was a dreadful thing among us to be out of Christ, in danger every day of dropping into hell. Indeed, the people were intent upon escaping for their lives and fleeing from the wrath to come (Matt. 3:7).

The people eagerly took every opportunity they could find for their souls. Very often they were inclined to meet together in private houses for religious purposes. Such meetings, when scheduled, were very crowded.

There was scarcely a single person in the town, old or young, left unconcerned about the great things of the eternal world. Those who were typically the vainest and loosest, and those who had been inclined to think and speak lightly of vital and practical religion, were now generally subject to great awakenings. The work of conversion was carried on in a most astonishing manner, and it increased more and more. Souls literally came by flocks to Jesus Christ. From day to day, for many months at a time, sinners were brought out of darkness into marvelous light (1 Pet. 2:9), delivered out of a horrible pit and from the miry clay, and set upon a rock with a new song of praise to God in their mouths (Ps. 40:2–3).

This work of God, as it went on and the number of true saints multiplied, soon made a glorious change in the town, so that in the following spring and summer of 1735, the town seemed to be full of the presence of God. It had never been so full of love and joy, and yet so full of distress, as it was then. There were remarkable signs of God's presence in almost every household. It was a time of joy in families because salvation had been brought to them: parents rejoiced over their children as if they had again been born, and husbands rejoiced over their wives, and wives over their husbands. The workings of God were then seen in His sanctuary (Ps. 68:24), the Lord's Day was a delight (Isa. 58:13), and His tabernacles were amiable (Ps. 84:1).

Our public assemblies were then beautiful; the congregation was alive in God's service, everyone earnestly intent on the public worship, every hearer eager to drink in the words of the minister as they came from his mouth. From time to time, the assembly in general were in tears while the Word was preached, some weeping with sorrow and distress, others with joy and love, others with pity and concern for the souls of their neighbors.

Our public praises were then greatly enlivened; God was then glorified by our singing of psalms *"in the beauty of holiness"* (Ps. 29:2). Scarcely any part of divine worship exceeded the singing of God's praises, during which good men among us have drawn forth grace and have had their hearts lifted up in the ways of God. Earlier, our congregation had excelled in everything I knew about the external part of worship. The men generally carried three parts of the music, and the women sang a part by themselves. But now, they were inclined to sing with unusual elevation of heart and voice, which made the duty pleasant indeed.

In all gatherings, on other days of the week and on whatever occasions people came together, Christ was to be heard of and seen in the midst of them. Our young people, when they met, were inclined to spend the time in talking of the excellency and dying love of Jesus Christ; the glory of the way of salvation; the wonderful, free, and sovereign grace of God; His glorious work in the conversion of a soul; the truth and certainty of the great things of God's Word; the sweetness of His perfections, and so on. Even at weddings, which formerly were mere occasions of mirth and frivolity, there was now no discourse about anything but religion, and there was no appearance of any happiness outside of the spiritual kind.

Those among us who had been formerly converted were greatly enlivened and renewed with fresh and extraordinary touches from the Spirit of God. Of course, some were affected much more than others, according to the measure of the gift of Christ. Many who before had labored under difficulties about their own state now had their doubts removed by more satisfying experiences and clearer discoveries of God's love.

THE WORK AFFECTS VISITORS TO THE TOWN

When this work first appeared and was so extraordinarily carried on among us in the winter, others around us seemed not to know what to make of it. Many scoffed at and ridiculed it, and some said that what we called conversion was comparable to certain mental disorders. However, it was very evident to many who occasionally visited us from abroad with careless and ignorant hearts, that what they saw here actually cured people of such disorders. Strangers were generally surprised to find things so much beyond what they had heard and were inclined to tell others that the state of the town could not be imagined by those who had not seen it.

It was very evident that the people who came to town when the circuit court sat in Northampton in the beginning of March also noticed the work of God here. Additionally, those who came from out of town to our public lectures were, for the most part, remarkably affected. Many who came to Northampton, on one occasion or other, had their consciences smitten and awakened; they went home with wounded hearts and with impressions that never wore off until they were saved.

Those who had serious thoughts beforehand had their awakenings and convictions greatly increased. There were many instances of people who came from abroad on visits or on business, who, before long, were remarkably saved and who partook of the shower of divine blessing that God rained down here. Indeed, many of them went home rejoicing. At length, the same work began to appear and prevail in several other towns in the region.

MANY SURROUNDING TOWNS ARE AFFECTED

In the month of March 1735, the people in South Hadley began to have deep concern about the things of religion, which very soon became universal. The work of God has been very wonderful there. In fact, in proportion to the size of the place, it has not been much less than what it has been here. About the same time, the work began to break forth in the west part of Suffield (where it also has been very great) and soon spread into all parts of the town. It appeared at Sunderland, also, and soon spread throughout the town; and I believe it was, for a season, not less remarkable there than it was here.

Around the same time, this great awakening began to appear in a part of Deerfield, called Green River, and afterwards filled the town. There has since been a glorious work there. It began also to be manifest in the south part of Hatfield, in a place called the Hill. The whole town, in the second week of April, seemed to be seized all at once with concern about the things of religion. The work of God has been great there. There has also been a very general awakening at West Springfield and Long Meadow, and in Enfield there was for a time a rather general concern among some who had before now been very loose in their behavior.

Around the time when this appeared at Enfield, the Rev. Bull of Westfield informed me that there had been a great change there and that more had been done in one week than had been done in the preceding seven years. Something of this work likewise appeared in the first precinct in Springfield, principally in the north and south extremes of the parish. And in Hadley, there gradually appeared a work of God that, at another time, would have been thought worthy of much notice. For a short time, there was also a very great and general concern of a similar nature at Northfield.

Wherever this concern appeared, it seemed not to be in vain. Rather, God brought saving blessings with Him in every place; and His Word, accompanied by His Spirit (as we have every reason to think), did not return void (Isa. 55:11). It might well have been said at that time, in all parts of the county, *"Who are these that fly as a cloud, and as the doves to their windows?"* (Isa. 60:8).

Other towns heard of this and found it to be a great means of awakening. When we heard of such a swift and extraordinary propagation and the extent of this work, it served to uphold the work among us for a time. The continual news kept the talk of religion alive, and it greatly quickened and gave joy to the hearts of God's people here. Those who saw themselves as still left behind were much awakened, and they became all the more earnest to share in the great blessings that others had obtained.

This remarkable outpouring of the Spirit of God thus extended from one end of this region to the other. It was not confined to Massachussets, but many places in Connecticut have also partaken in the same mercy. For instance, the first parish in Windsor, under the pastoral care of the Rev. Marsh, was thus blessed about the same time as we were in Northampton, while we had no knowledge of each other's circumstances.

There has been a very great ingathering of souls to Christ in Windsor, and a considerable sign of the same work began afterwards in East Windsor, my father's parish. East Windsor has in times past been favored with mercies of this nature, more than any on this western side of New England, excepting Northampton. There have been four or five seasons of the outpouring of the Spirit, to the general awakening of the people there, since the time when my father settled among them.

During the last spring and summer, there was also a wonderful work of God carried on at Coventry, under the ministry of the Rev. Meacham. I had the opportunity to converse with some Coventry people, who gave me a very remarkable account of the surprising changes that appeared in the rudest and most corrupt people there. The movement of God's hand was also very great at the same time in a part of Lebanon called the Crank, where the Rev. Wheelock, a young gentleman, has lately settled.

And there has been much of the same at Durham, under the ministry of the Rev. Chauncey, where there has been no small ingathering of souls. It is likewise among many of the young people in the first precinct in Stratford under the ministry of the Rev. Gould. The work in Stratford was greatly promoted by the remarkable conversion of a young woman who had been a great company-keeper, as it was here.

Something of this work also appeared in several other towns in that area, as I was informed when I was there last fall. Since then, we have been acquainted with something very remarkable of this nature at another parish in Stratford, called Ripton, under the pastoral care of the Rev. Mills. There was a considerable revival of religion last summer at New Haven, as I was once and again informed by the Rev. Noyes, the minister there, and by others. I very recently received a letter from Mr. Noyes, telling me of the revival there, and I have also heard of it from other sources.

This flourishing of religion still continues and has lately increased a great deal. Mr. Noyes wrote that many have been added to the church this summer, and he mentioned several young people in particular who belong to the principal families of that town. The same work has also been seen in the following towns in varying degrees: Guilford, in a small degree; Mansfield, under the ministry of the Rev. Eleazar Williams, in a very considerable degree; Tolland, with an unusual religious concern; and Hebron and Bolton, in small degrees.

The north parish in Preston, Connecticut, also witnessed a great effusion of the Spirit of God. I was informed of this, and saw a bit of it, when I was visiting the church of Rev. Lord last autumn. Rev. Lord, with the Rev. Owen from Groton, came here last May to see the work that God has been doing in Northampton. Having heard various and contradictory accounts of it, they took great care to settle the questions they had about the revival. Thus, they particularly conversed with many of our people, whom they declared to be entirely to their satisfaction.

Rev. Lord told me that, when he got home, he informed his congregation of what he had seen, and they were greatly affected by it. It proved to be the beginning of the same work among them. This work prevailed until there was a general awakening and many instances of people who were remarkably converted. I also have lately heard that there has been something of the work at Woodbury.

However, this shower of divine blessing has been even more extensive than this. Indeed, there was no small degree of it in some parts of New Jersey, as I was informed when I was in New York during a long journey I took at that time of the year for my health. Some people from New Jersey, whom I saw in New York, told me about it. The Rev. William Tennent, in particular, a minister who seemed to have such things at heart, told me of a very great awakening of many, in a place called the Mountains, under the ministry of Mr. Cross. In addition, Mr. Tennent told me about a very considerable revival of religion in another place under the ministry of his brother, the Rev. Gilbert Tennent. And, in another town, a revival was taking place under the ministry of a very pious young gentleman, a Dutch minister, whose name was Frelinghuysen.

Chapter 3

The Universality of God's Work

This revival among us seems to have been a very extraordinary dispensation of Providence. God has, in many respects, gone out of and far beyond His usual and ordinary way. The work in this town and others around us has been extraordinary on account of the universality of it, affecting all kinds of people, temperate and corrupt, high and low, rich and poor, wise and unwise. It has reached the most considerable families and individuals, as far as anyone can tell, as much as it has reached others.

In former stirrings of this nature, mostly young people have been affected. But now, old men and little children have been affected, too. Many children have, of their own accord, formed themselves into religious societies in different parts of the town. A loose, careless person could scarcely be found in the whole neighborhood. And, if there was anyone who seemed to remain unaware of or unconcerned with the things of religion, it would be spoken of as a strange thing.

This dispensation has also appeared extraordinary in the numbers of those on whom we have reason to think it has had a saving effect. We have about six hundred and twenty church members entitled to receive Communion, including almost all the adults. The church was very large before, but people never thronged into it as they did in the recent revival. Our Communion services are eight weeks apart, and I received into our membership about a hundred converts before one recent service. When eighty of them came at one time to make an open and explicit profession of Christianity, they were a moving sight for the rest of the congregation.

I took into our congregation nearly sixty people before the next Communion service, and I have very sufficient evidence of the conversion of their souls through divine grace. However, it is not the custom here, as it is in many other churches in this country, to base admission to the Lord's Supper upon a person's testimony of his own inward experiences.

I will not pretend that I am able to determine how many have been the subjects of such mercy. But, if I may declare what seems probable to me in a thing of this nature, I hope that more than three hundred souls were savingly brought home to Christ in this town in the period of half a year. Unlike years past, about the same number of males as females were affected. By what I have heard Rev. Stoddard say, this is very unusual, for he observed in his time that many more women were converted than men.

Many of the young people who are respected for reasons outside religion have become truly pious and are leading people in the ways of religion. Those who were formerly loose young people have generally become true lovers of God and Christ, and spiritual in their dispositions. I hope that the greater part of people above sixteen years of age in this town are the kind of people who have the saving knowledge of Jesus Christ. From what I have heard, I suppose it is so in some other places, particularly in Sunderland and South Hadley.

SPIRITUAL INFLUENCES ON BOTH OLD AND YOUNG

This has also appeared to be a very extraordinary dispensation in that the Spirit of God has extended not only His awakening, but also His regenerating influences, both to elderly persons and to those who are very young. Before now, it has been rare that anyone past middle age was converted. But now we have reason to think that as many older people have been savingly changed in this movement of God's Spirit as younger people have been in former years. I suppose there were more than fifty people converted in this town who were over forty years of age; more than twenty of them were above fifty, about ten of them above sixty, and two of them above seventy years of age.

Before now, it has been thought a strange thing when anyone has been savingly influenced by the Spirit's power and remarkably changed in his childhood. But now, I suppose, nearly thirty children between ten and fourteen years of age appeared to have been savingly changed. Two were between nine and ten, and one was about four years of age. I suppose it is difficult to believe that a four-year-old child could experience the effects of salvation, so in a later chapter I will give a detailed account of what happened with a young girl named Phebe Bartlet.

The influences of God's Holy Spirit have also been very remarkable on children in some other places, particularly at Sunderland, South Hadley, and the west part of Suffield. There are several families in this town who are all pious. Indeed, there are numerous families in which, I think, we have reason to hope that all the children are truly godly, and most of them have recently become so. There are very few houses in the whole town into which salvation has not lately come in one or more instances.

OTHER EXTRAORDINARY FEATURES

The Quickness of the Spirit

It also seems that God has gone out of His usual way in the quickness of this work, for His Spirit moved and operated swiftly in the hearts of many. It is wonderful that people have been so suddenly and yet so greatly changed. Many have been taken from a loose and careless way of living and seized with strong convictions of their guilt and misery, and in a very little time old things have passed away and all things have become new with them (2 Cor. 5:17).

The Extent of the Spirit's Influences

God's work has also appeared very extraordinary in the degrees of His influences. Many people have experienced high degrees of both awakening and conviction, and also of saving light, love, and joy.

The extent of the revival and the speed with which it has been propagated from town to town have also been very extraordinary. In former times of the outpouring of the Spirit of God on Northampton, though at times it was very remarkable, it reached no further then; the neighboring towns all around continued unmoved.

This work seemed to be at its greatest height in this town in the early part of the spring, in March and April. At that time, God's work in the conversion of souls was carried on among us in such a wonderful manner that, so far as I can judge, it appears to have been at the rate of at least four people a day, or nearly thirty in a week, for five or six weeks in a row. When God took the work into His own hands in such a remarkable manner, there was as much done in a day or two as was usually done in a year with all the effort and blessing that are usually allotted to men.

A Special Call to Record the Events

I am very much aware that many people, if they were to read the account I give here, would think that I enjoy exaggerating the matter. They will likely think that, for lack of sound judgment, I interpret every religious emotion and enthusiastic display of piety as saving conversion. I would not be surprised if they think so. For this reason, I have held back from publishing an account of this great work of God until now, though I have often been asked to write one.

But now, having a special call to give an account of it, upon mature consideration I thought it might be my duty to declare this amazing work and to conceal no part of the glory of it. I leave it up to God to take the credit for His own work, and I run the risk of any judgmental or prejudiced thoughts that might be directed toward me to my disadvantage. Moreover, so that people who have not seen this revival in person may have the advantage of judging it for themselves, I will now go into more extensive detail regarding the work that God has done here.

Chapter 4

The Nature of
Spiritual Conviction

The ways in which people have been converted are perhaps as numerous as the amount of people who have been affected by the Spirit's influences in this work. Nevertheless, most conversions carry a great similarity in many aspects, which I will describe here in this chapter.

AWARENESS OF A SINFUL CONDITION

People are first awakened when they sense their miserable natural condition and the danger they are in of perishing eternally. They suddenly feel that it is of great importance to them that they speedily escape and get into a better state. Those who were once secure and unaware of such things are made utterly aware of how much their former courses were leading them on the path to destruction.

Some people are convicted suddenly by the Spirit. When they hear the news of others' conversion, or when they hear something in public or private conversation, their consciences are smitten, and it is as if their hearts were pierced through with an arrow. Others are awakened more gradually. They become more pensive, so as to consider their case and to conclude that the best and wisest thing to do is to delay no longer, but to take advantage of the present opportunity. Accordingly, they have made it their practice to seriously meditate on things that have the tendency to awaken them and give them a deeper conviction. And so, their awakenings increase, until a sense of their misery has gotten hold of them by God's Holy Spirit setting in on their hearts.

Others who, before this wonderful time, had been somewhat religious and concerned about their salvation, have been awakened in a new manner. They have been made aware that their slack way of seeking God was never likely to attain that purpose.

The Effects of Being Awakened

These awakenings, when they have initially come upon people, have had two effects. First, people have been brought immediately to quit their sinful practices. Even the more corrupt sort have been led to forsake and regret their former vices and extravagances. Once the Spirit of God began to be so wonderfully poured out in a general way through Northampton, people soon put away their old quarrels, backbitings, and meddling with other people's concerns. The tavern was soon empty, and people kept very much at home. No one went out unless on necessary business or for some religious reason, and every day seemed in many respects like a Sabbath day.

The second effect of these awakenings was that they caused people to earnestly apply the means of salvation to their lives: reading, prayer, meditation, the ordinances of God's house, and private examination of Scripture. Their cry was, *"What must* [we] *do to be saved?"* (Acts 16:30). Their place for relaxation had changed; the minister's house was now thronged far more than the tavern ever had been likely to be.

SOME HAVE SUFFERED UNDER CONVICTION

Many people experience some degree of fear and trouble before they attain any comfortable evidences of pardon and acceptance with God. Some are, from the beginning, provided with abundantly more encouragement and hope than others. Some have had ten times less trouble of mind than others, in whom the result seems yet to be the same. Still others have had such a sense of the displeasure of God and the great danger they were in of damnation that they could not sleep at nights.

Many have said that when they have lain down, the thoughts of sleeping in such a condition have been frightful to them. In fact, they have scarcely been free from terror while asleep, and they have awakened with fear, heaviness, and distress still abiding in their spirits. It has been very common that the deep and persistent concern of people's minds has had a painful influence on their bodies. The awful images of misery have, for the most part, increased as people have gotten closer to deliverance. Their minds have undergone many changes. Sometimes they think themselves wholly senseless, and they fear that the Spirit of God has left them. They even fear that God has given them up to hardship and difficulty. Yet, they appear very deeply disquieted about these fears and are very eager to be convicted again.

Along with the rational fears and perplexity that they have considerable basis for, those under the conviction of sin have often suffered many needless distresses of thought. Satan probably has a great hand in these things, to entangle people's minds and to block their way to God. Sometimes depression has been evidently mixed in. When this happens, the Tempter seems to take great advantage of them and puts an obstacle of unhappiness in the way of any good effect. It is difficult to know how to deal with such people, because they twist everything that is said to them the wrong way, although they do so to their own disadvantage. There is nothing that the Devil seems to use against God's work more than an unhappy or depressed spirit, unless it is the real corruption of the heart.

However, it is very remarkable that there has been relatively little of this depression mixed in with conviction at this time of extraordinary blessing. In fact, there is more likelihood that people under awakenings at other times would have experienced depression in such a way. It is evident that many who had been very involved in such difficulties before, seemed now strangely to be set free of them. Some people who had been exceedingly entangled with peculiar temptations of one sort or another for a long time—with unprofitable and hurtful distresses—were soon helped over former stumbling blocks that hindered their progress toward salvation.

Indeed, convictions have had good results and have successfully carried people on in the path to life. In this way, Satan seemed to be restrained until near the end of this wonderful time, when God's Holy Spirit was about to withdraw.

Many times, people under great awakenings were concerned because they thought they were not awakened, but were still miserable, hardhearted, senseless, foolish creatures, standing on the brink of hell. Their sense of the need to be awakened and their awareness of their comparative hardness grew upon them with every awakening, so that they seemed to themselves to be very senseless, when indeed they were most sensible. There have been some instances of people who have had such a great sense of their danger and misery that a little more would probably have destroyed them. And yet, they have been much amazed at their own insensibility and dullness at such an extraordinary time.

People are sometimes brought to the edge of despair, and it looks as black as midnight to them a little before the day dawns in their souls. There have been several instances of individuals who have had such a sense of God's wrath for sin that they have been overcome by it and have cried out under an astonishing sense of their guilt. They wonder how God can allow such guilty wretches to live upon earth, and why He does not immediately send them to hell.

Sometimes their guilt stares them in the face in such a way that they are terrified that God will instantly send them to hell. But, more commonly, their distresses under legal awakenings have not been to such a degree. (When I say legal awakenings,

I am referring to those occasioned by looking into God's law.) In other people, when comfort has been very near, these terrors do not seem to be as sharp as before; their convictions have not led to terror so much as to a greater sense of their own universal depravity and deadness in sin.

The corruption of the heart has revealed itself in various ways in the time of legal conviction. Sometimes it appears in a great struggle, like something roused by an enemy; and Satan, the old inhabitant, seems to exert himself like a serpent disturbed and enraged. Many in such circumstances have felt a great spirit of envy toward the godly, especially toward those who have been recently converted, and most of all toward acquaintances and companions who have been converted.

Indeed, some have felt many heart-risings against God. They have murmured at His way of dealing with mankind, especially His dealings with themselves. Many have insisted, both in public and private, that people should have the utmost dread of such envious thoughts. For, if such thoughts are allowed, they tend to quench the Spirit of God, if not to provoke Him finally to forsake these individuals. When such a spirit of envy has long prevailed, and individuals have not earnestly fought against it as they should have, it has hindered the good of their souls.

Even so, in some other instances where people have been much terrified at the sight of such wickedness in their hearts, God has brought good to them out of evil. He has made evil a means of convincing them of their own desperate sinfulness and bringing them away from all self-confidence.

There have been some people who have not had great terrors, but they have had a very quick work. Some, who have not had such a deep conviction of these things before their conversion, have had much more of it afterwards. God is far from limiting Himself to any certain method when He convicts sinners of their sin. In some instances, it seems easy for our reasoning powers to discern how God deals with the soul under awakenings. In others, His footsteps cannot be traced (Ps. 77:19) and *"his ways* [are] *past finding out"* (Rom. 11:33).

The time of trouble varies from person to person. Some experience it for only a few days, and others for months or years. There were many in this town who, before this effusion of the Spirit upon us, had been concerned about their salvation for years. Although they were probably not thoroughly awakened, they were concerned to such a degree that they were very uneasy, so that they lived an uncomfortable, disquieted life. They continued to worry about their salvation, but they never obtained any comfortable evidence of a good state.

In this extraordinary time, several such individuals have received light, but many of them were some of the last to receive it. They saw multitudes of others rejoicing, with songs of deliverance in their mouths, who had earlier seemed wholly careless and at ease and in pursuit of vanity. They saw what wonderful things were happening to others, yet they remained anxious about their own souls. Indeed, some who had lived licentiously continued to do so until a little before they were converted, yet they soon came to rejoice in the infinite blessings God had bestowed upon them.

OTHER EFFECTS ACCOMPANYING CONVICTION

When the Spirit of God first begins to work in people's hearts, His tendency is to bring them to a conviction of their absolute dependence on His sovereign power and grace. He shows them their universal need for a Mediator. He does this by leading people more and more to a sense of their exceeding wickedness and guiltiness in His sight—to a sense of their pollution and the insufficiency of their own righteousness. He strives with them until they realize that they can in no way help themselves, and that God would be wholly just and righteous in rejecting them and all that they do, and in casting them off forever. Of course, there is a vast variety as to the manner and distinctness of such convictions.

As these people are gradually more and more convinced of the corruption and wickedness of their hearts, it seems to them that they grow worse and worse, harder and blinder, and more desperately wicked, instead of growing better. They are ready to be discouraged by it and oftentimes think that they have never been so far away from good, when in reality they are nearer than ever before. Under the awareness that the Spirit of God gives them of their sinfulness, they often think that they differ from everyone else. Their hearts are ready to sink with the thought that they are the worst of all, and that no one ever obtained mercy who was as wicked as they.

The Conscience Is Affected

When awakenings first begin, people's consciences are commonly most affected concerning their outward corruption or other acts of sin. Then, afterwards, they are much more burdened with a sense of inward heart sins, the dreadful corruption of their nature, their enmity against God, the pride of their hearts, their unbelief, their rejection of Christ, the stubbornness and obstinacy of their wills, and the like. In many, God makes much use of their own experiences, in the course of their awakenings and efforts toward salvation, to convince them of their own vile emptiness and universal depravity.

When people first begin to reflect on the past sin of their lives and begin to have a terrifying sense of God's anger, they very often vow to live more strictly, to confess their sins, and to perform many religious duties. All of this is done with a secret hope of appeasing God's anger and making up for the sins they have committed. Oftentimes, when first setting out, their consciences and their emotions are so moved that they are full of tears in their confessions and prayers. They are willing to place quite a bit of value in such prayers, as if they were some kind of atonement and had power to cause corresponding emotions in God, too.

Attempts and Disappointments Multiply

Hence, for a while they have high expectations of what God will do for them, and they imagine that they are quickly getting better and will soon be thoroughly converted. But, these feelings are short-lived; people quickly discover that they fail, and then they think themselves to be getting worse again. The prospect of being converted is not accomplished as quickly as they thought. Instead of being nearer, they seem to be farther off. They think their hearts have grown harder, and in this way their fears of perishing greatly increase.

Yet, although they are disappointed, they renew their attempts again and again, and as their attempts multiply, so do their disappointments. All fails, and they see no sign of having brought God's heart nearer to them. They do not see that He hears their prayers at all, as they expected He would. Sometimes great temptations have arisen to abandon seeking and to give up the whole case.

Wicked Thoughts against God

Nevertheless, they become more terrified with fears of perishing, and their former hopes of prevailing on God to be merciful to them in a great measure fail. Sometimes their religious emotions have turned into enmity against God because He apparently will not pity them and seems to have little regard for their distress and piteous cries, and for all the pains they go through. They think of the mercy that God has shown to others. How soon and how easily others have obtained comfort, those who were worse than they and who have not tried as hard as they have! Sometimes they have even had blasphemous thoughts in these circumstances.

But, when they reflect on these wicked thoughts against God—if their conviction is continued and the Spirit of God is not provoked to utterly forsake them—they have more distressing impressions of the anger of God toward those whose hearts remain so sinful. It may be that they have great fears of committing the unpardonable sin, or that God will surely never show mercy to these who are such vipers. They are often tempted to leave off the whole effort in despair.

More Disappointments

Yet, perhaps from something they read or hear about the infinite mercy of God or about the all-sufficiency of Christ for the chief of sinners, they have some encouragement, and hope is renewed. Even so, they think that they are still not fit to come to Christ; they are so wicked that Christ will never accept them. And then they may set themselves upon a new course of fruitless attempts to make themselves better in their own strength, and they will still meet with new disappointments. They earnestly wish to inquire what they must do. They wonder if there is something else to be done in order to obtain converting grace—something that they have never yet done.

Perhaps they hope that they are a little better than they were, but then the pleasing dream vanishes again. If they are told that they trust their own strength and righteousness too much, they cannot unlearn this practice all at once. They cannot yet find the appearance of any good, but everything looks as dark as midnight to them. Thus, they wander around from mountain to hill, *"seeking rest, and find*[ing] *none"* (Matt. 12:43). When they are thrown out of one refuge, they fly to another, until they are debilitated, broken, and subdued in humility. God gives them a conviction of their own utter helplessness and insufficiency, and He reveals the true remedy in a clearer knowledge of Christ and His Gospel.

Chapter 5

God's Justice and Grace in Convicting Sinners

When they first begin to seek salvation, people are usually profoundly ignorant of themselves. They are not aware of how blind they are and how little they can do toward bringing themselves to see spiritual things correctly. They do not understand how little they can do toward increasing and displaying holiness in their own souls. They are not aware of how remote they are from love for God and other holy inclinations, and how dead they are in sin. When they see unexpected pollution in their own hearts, they go about trying to wash away their own defilements to make themselves clean. By doing so, they weary themselves in vain, until God shows them that it is indeed in vain and that their help is not where they have sought it.

But some people continue wandering in such a labyrinth, ten times as long as others, before their own experience will convince them of their insufficiency. And so it appears to be not only their own experience, but also the convincing influence of God's Holy Spirit, that attains the effect. Recently,

God has abundantly shown that He does not need to convince men by long, fruitless, and often repeated trials. For, in multitudes of instances, He has convinced men more quickly. He has so awakened and convinced individuals' consciences, He has made them so aware of their great vileness, and He has given them such a sense of His wrath against sin, that He has quickly overcome all their vain self-confidence and has brought them down into the dust before a holy and righteous God.

GOD'S OBLIGATIONS TO MANKIND

Of course, God is under no obligation to show mercy to any natural man whose heart is not turned toward Him. It ought to be made clear to struggling souls that a man cannot challenge the absolute justice or the free promises of God, by pointing out anything he has done before he has believed on Jesus Christ or before true repentance has begun in him.

I have found that the sermons that have been most remarkably blessed are those concerning the doctrine of God's absolute sovereignty with regard to the salvation of sinners. He is just and righteous in answering the prayers and ending the pains of natural men. Out of all the sermons I have offered to my congregation, I never found one that could bring about the fruits of salvation so much as the words of Romans 3:19: *"That every mouth may be stopped."* Such a sermon attempts to show that it would be a just action on God's part to forever reject and cast off mere natural men.

It seems to me that, if I had taught any other doctrine to those who came to me under trouble, I would have taken a most direct course to utterly ruin them. I would have directly crossed what was clearly the direction of the Spirit of God in His influences upon them. For, if I were to tell them anything but the truth, it would have had either of two effects. First, it might have promoted self-flattery and carelessness, and so put an end to their awakenings. Or, secondly, it would have established their contention and strife with God concerning His dealings with them and others, and it would have blocked their way to being humbled before the Sovereign Giver of life and death.

God prepares individuals for His comforts when He humbles them. And yet, those who have been under awakenings have oftentimes plainly stood in need of being encouraged, by being told of the infinite and all-sufficient mercy of God in Christ. It is God's manner to cause diligence to prosper and to bless His own means, so that awakenings and encouragements, fear and hope, may be duly mixed and proportioned. In this way, people's minds are kept in a happy medium between the two extremes of self-flattery and despondence, both of which tend to lead to slackness and negligence and, in the end, to security in oneself, which is not security at all.

GOD'S SOVEREIGNTY IS SHOWN

When awakenings seem to have a saving result in certain individuals, commonly the first thing that appears after their legal troubles is a conviction of the justice of God in their condemnation. This appears in an awareness of their own exceeding sinfulness and the vileness of all their actions. In giving an account of this, the people of my congregation expressed themselves very diversely. Some said that they saw God was sovereign and might receive others, yet reject them. Some were convinced that God might justly bestow mercy on every other person in the town or in the world, and yet damn themselves to all eternity. Others claimed that they saw how God may justly give no regard to all the suffering they have undergone and all the prayers they have made.

Some said that if they were to look for God and to do so with great effort all their lives, God might justly cast them into hell even then, because all their labors, prayers, and tears could not make an atonement for the least sin or merit any blessing at the hands of God. Some declared themselves to be in the hands of God, that He might dispose of them just as He pleased. Others said that God might glorify Himself in their damnation, and they wondered why God had allowed them to live so long and had not cast them into hell long ago.

Some are brought to this conviction by a great sense of their general sinfulness, that they are such vile, wicked creatures in both heart and life. Others see the sins of their lives set before them in an extraordinary manner, multitudes of them coming fresh to their memory and being set before them with their additional evils. Some have their minds especially set on some particular wicked practice they have indulged. Some are especially convinced by a new knowledge of the corruption and wickedness of their hearts. Others see the horridness of some particular corruption that shows forth in the time of their awakening, by which the enmity of their heart against God is manifested. Some are especially convinced of their sinfulness by a sense of the sin of unbelief, the opposition of their hearts to the way of salvation by Christ, and their obstinacy in rejecting Him and His grace.

HOW GOD'S JUSTICE IS VIEWED

There is a great deal of difference in the distinctness of these awakenings. Some people who have not had such a clear sight of God's justice in their condemnation still mention things that plainly imply it. They develop a disposition to acknowledge that God is just and righteous in declaring that He will inflict punishment upon those who sin. They know that they are undeserving of His comforts. Many times, though they did not have such a clear sight of it at the beginning, they have very clear discoveries of their unworthiness soon after their conviction, along with great humblings in the dust before God.

Commonly, people's minds immediately before this discovery of God's justice are exceedingly restless, in a kind of struggle and tumult, and sometimes in anguish. But, generally, as soon as they have this conviction, it immediately brings their minds to a calm, unexpected quietness and composure. And, most frequently, though not always, the pressing weight upon their spirits is then taken away, and a general hope arises that sometime or other God will be gracious, even before any distinct and particular discoveries of mercy.

Often, they then conclude within themselves that they will lie at God's feet and wait for His timing. They rest in that, not being aware that the

Spirit of God has now brought them to a state in which they are prepared for mercy. It is remarkable that individuals, when they first have this sense of the justice of God, rarely think anything at the time of this being the humiliation they have often heard of and that others have experienced.

The first conviction that many people have concerning the justice of God in condemning them usually goes beyond anything found in the law of the Scriptures. Conviction may occur after humblings under the law and may arise from a sense of one's own helplessness and of the insufficiency of one's own duties, yet it does not appear to be forced by terrors and convictions that come by the law. Rather, the conviction of God's justice arises from a high exercise of grace, saving repentance, and evangelical humiliation.

Sometimes, at the discovery of the justice of God, sinners can scarcely hold back from crying out, "It is just! It is just!" Some say that they could see the glory of God shining bright in their own condemnation, and they are ready to think that if they are damned, they could join with God against themselves and would glorify His justice in that way. Thus, they commonly have an obvious sense of free and all-sufficient grace, though they can give no distinct account of it. Their awareness is manifested by the great degree of hope and encouragement that they then grasp, even though they were never as aware of their own vile and undeserving nature as they are at that time.

Some people in such circumstances have felt the excellency of God's justice in His vindictive displays of it against sinfulness such as their own. These people have so submitted to the idea of this attribute and of the displays of it—along with a great loathing of their own unworthiness and a kind of indignation against themselves—that they have sometimes almost called it a willingness to be damned. However, it must be acknowledged that they did not have very clear ideas of damnation, nor does any passage in the Bible require such self-denial as this. But, as some have more clearly expressed it, the truth is that salvation appeared too good for them, that they were worthy of nothing but condemnation, and that they could not tell how to think of salvation being bestowed upon them. They feared that salvation was inconsistent with the glory of God's majesty that they had so much scorned and defied.

GOD'S COMFORT COMES AFTER RECOGNIZING ONE'S SINFULNESS

Some people have found a great calmness of spirit after their distresses of conviction, and this tranquility continues for a while before any special and delightful manifestation of the grace of God—as it is revealed in the Gospel—is made to the soul. But, very often some comfortable and sweet view of a merciful God, of a sufficient Redeemer, or of some great and joyful things of the Gospel immediately follows, or follows in just a little time. For some people, the first sight of their just deserts of hell, their first image of God's sovereignty with respect to their salvation, and their discovery of all-sufficient grace are so near that they seem to go together.

These gracious discoveries, from which the first special comforts are derived, are quite varied in many respects. Frequently, Christ is distinctly made the focus of the mind, in His all-sufficiency and willingness to save sinners. However, some have their thoughts more especially fixed on God, in some of His sweet and glorious attributes manifested in the Gospel and shining forth in the face of Christ. Some see the all-sufficiency of the mercy and grace of God; some see chiefly the infinite power of God and His ability to save them and to do all things for them; and some look most at the truth and faithfulness of God.

In some people, the truth and certainty of the Gospel in general is the first joyful discovery they have; in others, the certain truth of some particular promise is first seen. In some, the grace and sincerity of God's call are discovered—commonly in some particular invitation in the mind—and it now appears real to them that God does indeed call them to Himself. Some are struck with the glory and wonderfulness of the dying love of Christ, and some with the sufficiency and preciousness of His blood, which was offered to atone for sin. Others discover the value and glory of Christ's obedience and righteousness. In some, the excellency and loveliness of Christ chiefly engages their thoughts; in others, it is His divinity, that He is indeed the Son of the living God. In still others, the excellency of the way of salvation by Christ and the suitableness of it to their needs are what convinces them.

Oftentimes some particular text of Scripture in the mind holds forth some evangelical basis for consolation. Sometimes a multitude of texts, gracious invitations and promises flowing in one after another, fill the soul more and more with comfort and satisfaction. Comfort is first given to some people while they are reading some portion of Scripture.

However, in some, comfort is accompanied by no particular Scripture at all, either in reading or meditation. In some, many divine things seem to be revealed to the soul all at once, or so it seems. Others have their minds especially fixed on one thing at first, and afterwards a sense of other things is given. In some this occurs swiftly, and in others it is a slower process, sometimes with interruptions of much darkness.

Grace Is Given

After humiliation by the law, grace sometimes seems to appear in earnest longings for God and Christ: to know God, to love Him, to be humble before Him, to have communion with Christ in His benefits. These longings, so it is claimed, seem to arise from a sense of the superlative excellency of divine things, along with a spiritual taste and relish for them and an esteem of them as a person's highest happiness and best portion. Such longings are commonly accompanied by firm resolutions to pursue this good forever, along with a hoping, waiting disposition. When people have begun in such states of mind, commonly other experiences and discoveries have soon followed, which have yet more clearly manifested a change of heart.

It ought to be acknowledged that Christ is not always distinctly and explicitly thought of in the first acts of grace upon a person's soul, though most commonly He is. Instead, He is sometimes only the implicit focus of the mind. Thus, when people have evidently been stripped of all their own righteousness and have condemned themselves as guilty of death, they have been comforted with a joyful and satisfying view that the mercy and grace of God are sufficient for them. They are comforted by the knowledge that their sins, though never so great, will not hinder their acceptance with God.

A Sense of God's Mercy through Christ

These individuals know that there is enough mercy in God for the whole world. They give no account of any particular or distinct thought of Christ; yet, when the account they give is duly weighed and they are questioned about it, it seems that the revelation of mercy in the Gospel is the basis for their encouragement and hope. Indeed, they discover that God's mercy is found entirely in relying on Christ and is not in any way initiated by anything in themselves.

Sometimes disconsolate souls have been revived and brought to rest in God by a sweet sense of His grace and faithfulness. This often happens through some special invitation or promise. However, there is again no particular mention of Christ in it, nor is it accompanied by any distinct thought of Him in their minds. Yet, it is not received as out of Christ, but as one of the invitations or promises made by God to poor sinners through His Son Jesus. Such people afterwards have had clear and distinct discoveries of Christ, accompanied by lively and special displays of faith and love toward Him.

Joy and Refreshment

It has more frequently happened that, when people have first had the Gospel of relief revealed to them and have entertained the sweet prospect it holds, they have thought nothing at that time of being converted. Yet, when they see that God is all-sufficient and has made plentiful provision for us in Christ, and after they have been humbled with a sense of their guilt and fears of wrath, they are greatly refreshed. The view is joyful to them, for it is glorious; it gives them new and more delightful ideas of God and Christ, and it greatly encourages them to seek conversion.

This begets in them a strong resolution to devote themselves entirely to God and His Son, and to patiently wait until God sees fit to make everything according to His desire. Additionally, they very often entertain a strong persuasion that He will do it for them in His own time. A holy repose in God through Christ begins in their souls, with a secret disposition to fear and love Him, and to hope for blessings from Him in this way. Yet, they have no idea that they are now converted; it does not so much as come into their minds.

IDEAS ABOUT SALVATION

Very often this occurs because they do not understand that, by their obedient and joyful entertainment of this discovery of grace, they have actually accepted the sufficiency of the salvation that they behold in Christ. They do not know that the sweet complacence they feel in God's mercy and salvation—which include pardon and sanctification and are held forth to them only through Christ—is a true receiving of this mercy, or a plain evidence of their receiving it. They expected some sort of action to take place in their souls, and perhaps they had no distinct idea themselves of what it would be.

Indeed, it is quite obvious in some of them that before their own conversions they had very imperfect ideas of what conversion is. It is all new and strange, for there was no clear conception of these things before. It is entirely evident, as they themselves acknowledge, that the expressions used to describe conversion and the graces of God's Holy Spirit—such as "a spiritual sight of Christ," "faith in Christ," "poverty of spirit," "trust in God," and so on—did not help them to understand in their minds what was meant by such words. Perhaps to some of them such expressions were little more than the names of colors are to one who is blind from his birth.

In this town there has always been a great deal of talk about conversion and spiritual experiences. Therefore, people in general had formed in their own minds an idea of what these things were. However, when they came to experience such things, they found themselves very confused, and many of their former ideas had to be overthrown. It has been very obvious to many that people of the greatest understanding, who had studied the most about things of this nature, have been more confounded than others.

Some of these theologians declare that all their former wisdom has come to mean nothing, and that they seem to have been mere babes who knew nothing. It has seemed to them that no one has stood more in need of instruction, even from their fellow Christians, concerning their own circumstances and difficulties than themselves. Seemingly with delight, they have seen themselves thus brought down and turned to nothing, so that free grace and divine power may be exalted in them.

AN EMOTIONAL EXPERIENCE

It was very wonderful to see how people's emotions were moved and influenced when God suddenly opened their eyes and gave them a sense of the greatness of His grace, the fullness of Christ, and His readiness to save. After having been broken with impressions of divine wrath, they sank into an abyss under a sense of guilt that they were ready to think was beyond the mercy of God. Their joyful surprise has caused their hearts to leap, so that they have been ready to break forth into laughter, tears often at the same time coming forth like a flood. And they have wept with loud cries. Sometimes they have not been able to hold back from crying out with a loud voice, expressing their great admiration.

The view of the glory of God's sovereignty and grace has surprised the souls of others with such sweetness that it has produced the same effects. I remember an instance of one who, after reading something concerning God's sovereign way of saving sinners, felt a sudden rapture of joy and delight in the consideration of it. This person saw that God is self-moved; the righteousness of man is not the motive for God's grace. Rather, man's imputed righteousness magnifies God and puts man even lower. And yet, after coming to this knowledge, this individual suspected himself to be in a Christless condition and had for a long time been in great distress for fear that God would not have mercy on him.

Many people continue to experience such grace for a long time and yet do not think themselves to be converted. Instead, they conclude the opposite. No one knows how long they would continue this way if they were not helped by particular instruction. There are undoubted instances of some who have lived in this state for many years. These circumstances of being converted and not believing it have had various consequences for different people, and sometimes the same people would experience different consequences.

A GREATER AWARENESS OF SIN

Some people continue to hope that they will obtain mercy by seeking it with strong perseverance and by humbly waiting for it before God. But very often, when the lively sense of the sufficiency of Christ and the riches of divine grace begins to vanish—when divine influences seem to withdraw themselves—they fall into greater distress than ever before. For they now have a far greater sense of the misery of the natural condition than before, having become newly aware of the reality of eternal things, the greatness of God, His excellency, and how dreadful it is to be separated from Him and to be subject to His wrath. Indeed, they are sometimes swallowed up with darkness and amazement because of it all.

Satan has a great advantage in such cases to manipulate people with various temptations, which he is not likely to neglect. In such a case, people very much need a guide to lead them to an understanding of what we are taught in the Word of God concerning the nature of grace, and to help them to apply it to themselves.

For many people, grace has been like the trees in winter or like seed in the springtime, suppressed under a hard clod of earth. Through an ignorance of their condition, and by seeing themselves still as the objects of God's displeasure, many have tried to their utmost to divert their minds from the pleasing and joyful views they have had. They have tried to suppress those consolations and gracious emotions that arose from the knowledge they received. And when it has entered into their minds to inquire whether or not this was true grace, they have been very afraid, lest they might be deceived with common illuminations and flashes of holy affections, and thereby eternally ruined with a false hope.

But when they have been better instructed and begin to allow themselves to have hope, this has awakened the gracious disposition of their hearts into life and vigor. It is as if the warm beams of the sun in the springtime have quickened the seeds and yields of the earth. Grace, when it is finally free and cherished with hope, soon flows out to their abundant satisfaction and increase.

Chapter 6

The Conversion Experience

There is no one thing that I know of that God has used more to promote His work among us than the news of others' conversion. Awakened sinners have desired to seek the same blessing. Though I have thought that a minister might be justified in declaring his judgment about particular individuals' experiences, I often signify to my congregation how unable man is to know another's heart, and how unsafe it is to depend merely on the judgment of others. I have often insisted that the fruits of sincerity are better than any manifestation they can make of it in words alone. Without bringing forth such fruit, all claims of spiritual experiences are in vain. My entire congregation can attest to my position on this.

The people in general, in this extraordinary time, have shown an extraordinary fear of being deceived. They are fearful lest they should progress wrongly. Some of them have been reluctant to receive hope, even to a great extreme.

I have been blamed and judged by many for making it my practice to signify to certain people my satisfaction with their condition. This has been greatly misrepresented abroad, along with innumerable other things concerning this revival, to set the country against the whole affair. But, let it be noted that in such cases I have tried to examine people's testimonies rather than to approve of the people themselves. I have certainly not neglected my duty as a pastor to assist and instruct people in applying Scripture to their own cases (in which, I think, many greatly need a guide). Yet, where the case seemed clear, I have taken the liberty of expressing to others my hopes for certain individuals. Nevertheless, I have been far from doing this concerning all for whom I have had such hopes.

I believe I have used much more caution than many have supposed. Even so, I consider it a great calamity to be deprived of the comfort of rejoicing with those of my flock who have been in great distress, whose circumstances I have been acquainted with, when there seems to be good evidence that those who were dead are alive and that those who were lost are found (Luke 15:24). I am aware that the practice would have been safer in the hands of someone with a riper judgment and greater experience, yet there seems to be an absolute need for it in the aforementioned accounts. It has been found to be something that God has most remarkably blessed among us, both to the people themselves and to others.

Conversion is a great and glorious work of God's power, at once changing the heart and infusing life into the dead soul, though the grace implanted at that time more gradually displays itself in some than in others. However, if one tries to determine the exact time when new converts show forth the very first act of grace, there is a great deal of difference among people. In some, the exact moment seems to be very discernible, but others are more at a loss. In this respect, there are very many who do not know, even when they have it, that it is the grace of conversion. Sometimes they do not think it to be so until a long time afterward.

THE BEGINNING OF CONVERSION

Many people, even when they begin to entertain great hopes that they are converted, are unsure about their actual conversion experience. Even if they remember what they experienced in the first glimpses of grace, they are still at a loss. Sometimes they question whether it was any more than a common illumination. Or they wonder whether some other clearer and more remarkable experience, which they had later on, was not the first to have had a saving influence upon their souls. The manner of God's work on the soul is sometimes especially mysterious, and it is up to God to determine how it will be manifested in the heart of a convert.

> *So is the kingdom of God, as if a man should cast seed into the ground; and should sleep, and rise night and day, and the seed should spring and grow up, he knoweth not how. For the earth bringeth forth fruit of herself; first the blade, then the ear, after that the full corn in the ear.* (Mark 4:26–28)

In some, converting light is like a glorious brightness suddenly shining upon a person and everyone around him. In a remarkable manner, they are brought out of darkness into marvelous light (1 Pet. 2:9). In many others, it has been like the dawning of the day, when a little light appears, though it may soon be hidden by a cloud. Then it appears again and shines a little brighter and gradually increases amid the darkness, until finally the light breaks forth more clearly from behind the clouds.

Many people are certainly ready to put the wrong date on their conversion, throwing aside the lesser degrees of light that first appeared at the dawn and claiming that their conversion took place with some more remarkable experience that they had afterwards. This often arises from a wrong understanding of what they have always been taught—that conversion is a great change, in which *"old things are passed away...*[and] *all things are become new"* (2 Cor. 5:17).

SCRIPTURE AND THE SPIRIT'S INFLUENCE

When they are first converted—and even afterwards—people commonly have had many verses of Scripture brought to their minds, verses that are suitable to their circumstances. These verses often come with great power, as the Word of God and of Christ. Many have a multitude of sweet invitations, promises, and praises flowing in one after another, bringing great light and comfort with them, filling the soul to the brim, enlarging the heart, and opening the mouth in religion. It seems necessary to suppose that there is often an immediate influence of the Spirit of God in bringing these verses of Scripture to the mind.

I do not suppose this happens through immediate revelation without any use of the memory. However, there seems to be an obvious, immediate, and extraordinary influence that leads their thoughts to such and such passages of Scripture, activating them in the memory. Indeed, in some people, God seems to bring passages of Scripture to their minds in no other way than by leading them into states of mind and meditations that harmonize with those Scriptures. In many people, there seems to be something more than just remembering a verse or two.

NOTICEABLE CHANGES AND EFFECTS

Those who have had the greatest terrors while under convictions of the law have not always obtained the greatest light and comfort. Nor have they always had light suddenly communicated. Yet, the time of conversion has generally been most perceptible in such people. Oftentimes the first noticeable change after the extreme terrors is a calmness, and then the light gradually comes in. At first there are small glimpses of the light after their midnight darkness and a word or two of comfort, as it were, softly spoken to them. They have a little taste of the sweetness of divine grace and the love of a Savior, when terror and distress of conscience begin to turn into a humble, meek sense of their own unworthiness before God.

Sometimes these people experience an inward inclination to praise God, and after a little while the light comes in more clearly and powerfully. Yet, more frequently, great fears have been followed by greater and more sudden light and comfort. When the sinner seems to be subdued and brought to a calm state, after having so much trouble of mind, then God lets in an extraordinary sense of His great mercy through a Redeemer.

Extraordinary Certainty about Religion

Converting influences very commonly bring an extraordinary conviction of the reality and certainty of the great things of religion. Of course, in some people this is much greater sometime after conversion than it was at first. They see and taste of the divine excellency of the Gospel, which more effectively convinces them than reading many volumes of arguments about it. It seems to me that in many instances, when the glory of Christian truths has been set before a person and he has at the same time seen and tasted and felt the divinity of them, he is as far from doubting their truth as he is from doubting whether there is a sun when his eyes are open under a clear sky.

Indeed, the strong blaze of God's light overcomes all objections. And yet, many of these people, if we were to ask them why they believed those things to be true, would not be able to well express or communicate a sufficient reason to satisfy our inquiries. Perhaps they would make no other answer but that they see God to be true. Even so, if someone were to have a deeper conversation with these new converts, he would be satisfied that, by their answer, they mean to say that they have intuitively beheld and immediately felt the most illustrious works and the powerful evidence of divinity in them.

In this way, some are convinced of the truth of the Gospel in general and that the Scriptures are the Word of God. Others set their minds more especially on some particular doctrine of the Gospel, or upon some particular truth that they are meditating on or reading about in some portion of Scripture. Some have such conviction in a much more remarkable manner than others. And there are some who never before had such a special sense of the certainty of divine things impressed upon them with such inward evidence and strength.

Outward Signs of Grace

The latter also have very clear displays of grace—of love for God, repentance, and holiness. And if they are more particularly examined, they clearly appear to have been inwardly convinced of the reality of divine things, though they were not quite so persuaded of these things before their conversion.

Those who have the clearest discoveries of divine truth in the manner that has been mentioned, cannot always have them in view. When the sense and relish of the divine excellency of these things fade, when the Spirit of God seems to withdraw, they do not have their conviction of the truth at command. In a dull state of mind, they cannot perfectly recall the idea and inward sense they had; things appear very dim when compared with how they looked before. There still remains a strong, habitual persuasion in them, yet not to such a degree that temptations to unbelief are excluded or that all possibility of doubting is erased.

Reasoning Powers Lead to a Sense of the Truth

But then, by God's help, the same sense of things revives again at particular times, like fire that lay hidden in ashes. The grounds of such a conviction of the truth of divine things is just and rational; yet God makes use of the minds of some much more obviously than He does in others. Oftentimes people have (as far as others can tell) received the first saving conviction from reasonings that they have heard from the pulpit, and often in the course of such reasoning they are led into their own meditations.

The arguments are the same ones that they have heard hundreds of times, but the force of the arguments, and their conviction by them, is altogether new. The words come with a new and previously unexperienced power. Before, they heard it was so, and they allowed it to be so; but now they see it to be so indeed. Things now look exceptionally clear to them, and they wonder how they did not see them before. They are so greatly taken with their new discovery, and things appear so clear and so rational to them, that they are often at first ready to think they can convince others. They are likely to engage in talk with nearly everyone they meet, in order to convince them. And when they are disappointed, they are ready to wonder why their reasonings seem to make no more impression on their souls.

Many make the mistake of doubting their saved condition because so much of their own reason—not God's or anyone else's—was used in the convictions they have received. They are afraid that they have no illumination beyond the natural force of their own faculties. Therefore, they turn this into an objection against the spirituality of their convictions. How can it be so easy to see things as they now see them? They have often heard that conversion is a work of mighty power, manifesting to the soul what neither man nor angel can convince us of. But it seems to them that these things are so plain and easy and rational that anybody can see them. If they are asked why they never saw things this way before, they say it was because they never thought of it.

Nevertheless, these difficulties are very often soon removed by those of another nature. For when God withdraws, they find themselves blind again, and they temporarily lose their sense of those things that looked so clear to them. No matter what they do, they cannot recover it until God renews the influence of His Spirit.

EVERYTHING RELIGIOUS SEEMS NEW

After their conversion, people often say that religious things seem new to them, that preaching is a new thing, that it seems as though they never heard preaching before, that the Bible is a new book, that they find new chapters and new psalms and new histories in it because they see them in a new light. A remarkable instance of this occurred with an aged woman, about seventy years old, who had spent most of her days under Rev. Stoddard's powerful ministry.

Reading in the New Testament concerning Christ's sufferings for sinners, she seemed astonished at what she read. It all seemed real and very wonderful, but also quite new to her. At first, before she had time to consider the meaning of the passage, she wondered why she had never heard of it before. But then she immediately collected herself, and she knew that she had often heard of it and read of it, but never until now had she seen it as real.

She then considered in her mind how amazing this was, that the Son of God underwent such things for sinners, yet how she had spent her time in ungrateful sin against so good a God and against such a Savior. This is what she thought, though she was apparently a person of a very blameless and inoffensive life. And she was so overcome by those considerations that she was ready to faint because of them. Those who were around her and did not know what was the matter were surprised and thought she was dying.

DELIGHTFUL THOUGHTS

Many people have said a great deal about their hearts being drawn out in love for God and Christ. They have spoken about their minds being wrapped up in delightful contemplation of the glory and wonderful grace of God, the excellency and dying love of Jesus Christ. And they have told how their souls have gone forth in desire for God and Christ. Several of our young children have expressed much of this and have shown a willingness to leave father and mother and all things in the world, to go and be with Christ. Some people have had such desires for Christ, or these desires have risen to such degree, that their natural strength has been taken away and they have fainted.

Some have been so overcome with a sense of the dying love of Christ to such poor, wretched, and unworthy creatures that their bodies have grown weak. Several people have had such a great sense of the glory of God and the excellency of Christ that nature and life seemed almost to sink under it. In all probability, if God had showed them a little more of Himself, it would have taken all life from their bodies.

I have seen and conversed with some of these people whose bodies have weakened, who have certainly been perfectly sober and very far from anything wild or fanatical. When able to speak, they have talked of the glory of God's perfections, the wonderfulness of His grace in Christ, and their own unworthiness, and they have done so in such a manner that no one else can express it as they did. Their sense of their extraordinary littleness and vileness, and their inclination to completely humble themselves before God, has appeared to be great in proportion to their light and joy.

Chapter 7

God's Glorious Work of Salvation

Those among us who have been set apart by the most extraordinary revelations and discoveries have seldom appeared with the assuming, conceited, and self-sufficient airs of enthusiasts, but quite the contrary. These people are noted for a spirit of meekness, modesty, lack of trust in themselves, and a humble opinion of themselves. No one appears as aware of his need for instruction and so eager to receive it as some of them, nor is anyone else so ready to think others better than themselves. Those who have been considered as converted among us have generally manifested a longing to lie low and in the dust before God. Indeed, they have even complained about not being able to lie low enough.

New converts very often talk about their awareness of the excellency of salvation by free and sovereign grace, through the righteousness of Christ alone. They describe how they renounce their own righteousness with delight and rejoice in having no account made of it. Many have said that it would lessen the satisfaction they hope for in heaven to have salvation by their own righteousness, or in any other way than by God's gift of free grace and for Christ's sake alone.

THE JOY OF ASSURANCE

They speak much about the inexpressible nature of what they experience; they tell how their words fail, so that they cannot declare it. They speak with great admiration for the superlative excellency of the pleasure and delight that they sometimes enjoy. Just a little of it, they say, is sufficient to pay them for all the pains and trouble they have gone through in seeking salvation, and it greatly exceeds all earthly pleasures. Some express how their spiritual awareness now allows them to see the vanity of earthly enjoyments, how mean and worthless all these things appear.

Many, while their minds have been filled with spiritual delights, have forgotten about eating; their bodily appetites have failed, while their minds have been entertained with *"meat to eat that* [others] *know not of"* (John 4:32). The light and comfort that some of them enjoy give a new relish to their common blessings and cause all things around them to appear beautiful, sweet, and pleasant. All things abroad—the sun, moon, and stars, the clouds and sky, the heavens and earth—appear with a divine glory and sweetness upon them.

This joy includes a delightful sense of the safety of their own condition. Yet, frequently, in times of their highest spiritual joys, this seems not to be the chief focus of their thought and meditation. The highest attention of their minds is on the glorious excellencies of God and Christ. There is very often a ravishing sense of God's love accompanying a sense of His excellency. They rejoice in a sense of the faithfulness of God's promises with respect to the future eternal enjoyment of Him.

The unparalleled joy of which they speak is the joy they find when they are lowest in the dust, emptied most of themselves, and annihilating themselves before God; when they are nothing, and God is all; when they see their own unworthiness, depend not at all on themselves, but alone on Christ, and ascribe all glory to God. Then their souls enjoy a satisfying rest, except that they see themselves as not sufficiently self-abased at such times. For then, above all other times, they desire to be lower. Some speak much of the exquisite sweetness and rest for the soul that is to be found in resignation to God and humble submission to His will.

Many express earnest longings of their souls to praise God, but at the same time complain that they cannot praise Him as they wish to. They want to have others help them in praising Him, and they are ready to call upon everything to praise Him. They express a desire to live to God's glory and to do something to His honor, but at the same time complain of their insufficiency and barrenness. They complain that they are poor and impotent creatures, can do nothing of themselves, and are utterly insufficient to glorify their Creator and Redeemer.

A CHANGE IN OUTLOOK

While God was so remarkably present among us by His Spirit, there was no book as delightful as the

Bible, especially the book of Psalms, the prophecy of Isaiah, and the New Testament. Some, because of their love for God's Word, at times have been wonderfully delighted and affected at the sight of a Bible. Also, there was no time so prized as the Lord's Day, and no place in this world so desired as God's house. Our converts then remarkably appeared united in dear affection for one another, and many have expressed much of that spirit of love which they felt toward all mankind, particularly to those who had been least friendly to them in the past.

I believe that more was done in the last year than ever before to confess injuries and to make up differences. After their own conversion, people have commonly expressed a great desire for the conversion of others. Some have thought that they would be willing to die for the conversion of even the meanest of their fellow creatures, or of their worst enemies. Indeed, many have been in great distress over the condition of others' souls. This work of God has also increased people's affections toward their ministers.

There are some people with whom I have been acquainted who belong to other towns and have been swallowed up with a sense of the awesome greatness and majesty of God. There are two of such people in particular, and both of them told me that, if, at the time of God's work upon their hearts, they had had the least fear that they were not at peace with so great a God, they would certainly have died.

It is worth saying that some people, by being converted, seem to be greatly helped in their doctrinal notions of religion. It was particularly remarkable in one person who was raised in Canada as a Catholic. Several years later he returned to his homeland and was partly drawn away from Catholicism, but he seemed very awkward and could hardly receive any clear notion of the Protestant scheme until he was converted. Then, he was remarkably altered in this respect.

EXPERIENCES DIFFER, BUT GOD IS THE SAME

There is a vast difference in the degree and manner of people's experiences, both at and after conversion. Some have grace working more tangibly in one way, others in another. Some speak more fully of a conviction of the justice of God in their condemnation, while others tell more about their consenting to the way of salvation by Christ. Others say more about their displays of love for God and Christ.

Some speak more about a sweet and assured conviction of the truth and faithfulness of God in His promises. Others say much about choosing and resting in God as their whole and everlasting portion. Their ardent desire for God, to have communion with Him, is prominent in their conversation. Others talk frequently about their abhorrence of themselves for their past sins and about their earnest longings to live for God's glory from then on.

Although the experiences differ from person to person, it seems to be the same work, the same habitual change, brought about in the heart. It all leads to the same end, and it is plainly the same Spirit that breathes and acts in the various people. There is an endless variety in the manner and circumstances in which people are changed. This is an opportunity to see that God does not, as some imagine, confine Himself to a particular method in His work on souls. I believe it has caused some people among us, who were before too ready to make their own experience a rule for others, to be less judgmental and more generous with their benevolence.

This is an excellent advantage indeed. The work of God has been glorious in its variety. It has displayed the manifold and unsearchable wisdom of God and brought about more charity among His people.

VARYING DEGREES OF ASSURANCE

Among those who have been converted, there are also many different degrees of hope and satisfaction concerning their condition. Some have a high degree of satisfaction in this matter almost all the time. Yet, it is rare that anyone enjoys such a full assurance of his interest in Christ that self-examination seems unnecessary. However, it may seem unnecessary to them when they are experiencing the actual enjoyment of some great revelation of God's glory and rich grace in Christ.

The majority of the people, as they sometimes fall into dead states of spirit, are frequently tried with fears concerning their condition. They generally have an awful impression of the dreadful nature of a false hope, and most are very cautious, lest in giving an account of their experiences they should say too much and use terminology that is too strong. Many, after they have related their experiences, have been greatly afflicted with fears, lest they have played the hypocrite and used stronger terms than their case would fairly allow. Even so, they could not think of how they could correct themselves.

Corruption Remains in the Heart

I think the main basis of the doubts and fears that people have had about their own state after their conversion, has been that they have found so much corruption remaining in their hearts. At first, their souls seem to be all alive, their hearts are fixed, and their holy affections are flowing. They seem to live quite above the world, and they encounter little difficulty in their religious practices. They are ready to think it will always be so easy.

People are truly abased under a sense of their vileness because of former acts of sin, yet they are not sufficiently aware of the corruption that still remains in their hearts. Therefore, they are surprised to find themselves in dull and dead spiritual states, troubled by wandering thoughts during the time of public and private worship, and utterly unable to keep themselves from such thoughts. They sometimes find themselves unaffected when there is the greatest occasion to be affected. And when they feel worldly dispositions working in them—pride, envy, stirrings of revenge, or some bad feeling toward someone who has injured them, as well as other workings of indwelling sin—their hearts are almost sunk with the disappointment. By then, they are ready to think that they are mere hypocrites.

They are prepared to argue that, if God had indeed done such great things for them as they hoped, their ingratitude would be inconsistent with

His grace. They complain of the hardness and wickedness of their hearts; they say there is so much corruption that it seems impossible to them that there should be any goodness there. Many of them seem to be much more aware now of how corrupt their hearts are, than before they were converted. And some have too easily begun to fear that, instead of becoming better, they grow much worse.

They make this an argument against the goodness of their state. But, in truth, they are only feeling the pain of their own wound. They have a watchful eye that they did not have before upon their own hearts. They take more notice of the sin that is there, which is now more burdensome to them, and they strive more against it, feeling more of its strength.

Not What Had Been Expected

They are somewhat surprised to find their situation so different from the idea they generally had about godly people. For, though grace is indeed of a far more excellent nature than they imagined, those who are godly have much less of it and much more remaining corruption than they thought. They never realized that individuals were likely to meet with such difficulties after they are converted. When they have doubts about their condition because of the deadness of their spiritual state, they are commonly unable to convince themselves of the truth of their grace as long as they remain in this state. All their self-examination does not seem to satisfy them.

When they hear about the signs of grace that ought to be seen in people after conversion, they are often so clouded that they do not know how to apply these signs to themselves. They hardly know whether they have such things or not, or whether they have experienced them or not. They cannot recover a sense of the sweetest, best, and most distinguishing aspects of their experiences. But, when the influences of the Spirit of God return to revive grace in them, the light breaks through the cloud, and doubting and darkness soon vanish away.

Godly Conversation and Scripture

People are often revived out of their dead and dark states by religious conversation. While they are talking about divine things, their souls are carried away into holy exercises with abundant pleasure. And oftentimes, while relating their past experiences to their fellow Christians, they have a sense of being revived, and the same experiences are in a degree renewed again.

Sometimes, while people are struggling with questions about the goodness of their state, Scriptures will come to their minds one after another in answer to their difficulties. Such Scriptures are highly pertinent to their circumstances. By this means, their darkness is scattered. Often, especially after long-continued deadness and dark states of mind, there are renewed humblings before any new remarkable comfort is given. The great sense of their own exceeding vileness and unworthiness is renewed, as it was before their first comforts were bestowed.

SALVATION IS SUPERNATURAL

Many people in the country have held low opinions about this great work, mostly because of what they have heard about impressions made on people's minds. However, there have been great misrepresentations and innumerable false reports concerning this matter. It is not, that I know of, the opinion of any one person in this town that any significance is to be attributed to anything seen with the natural eyes. In fact, the opposite is a received and established principle among us. I cannot say that there have been no instances of individuals who have been ready to give too much heed to vain and useless imaginings, but they have been easily corrected.

It should not be any mystery that a congregation might need a guide in such cases, to assist them in distinguishing the wheat from the chaff. But the more common impressions on people's minds are nothing but what is to be expected in human nature in such circumstances. They are the natural result of the strong exercise of the mind and impressions on the heart.

I do not suppose that they themselves imagine they saw anything with their natural eyes. Rather, they have had ideas strongly impressed within them, and lively images in their minds. For instance, through fear of hell, some people have had ideas of a dreadful furnace. Others, when their hearts have been strongly impressed and their emotions greatly moved with a sense of the beauty and excellency of Christ, have had such great impressions made on their minds that, along with a sense of His glorious spiritual perfections, there has been the image of

One who stands in glorious majesty with a sweet and gracious appearance.

Some people, when they are greatly moved by thoughts of Christ's death, have at the same time a vivid impression of Christ hanging upon the cross and His blood running from His wounds. Surely such things cannot be wondered at when so many earthly matters often bring forth lively ideas and pictures in the mind.

THE SPIRITUAL VERSUS THE IMAGINARY

Confusion over these matters is perhaps likely to fill some people's minds with imaginary ideas more so than others. This probably arises from a difference in physical makeup as well as from a difference in people's particular circumstances. When individuals have gone through extreme terrors, and when there is a sudden change to light and joy, the imagination seems more receptive to strong ideas. The lesser mental faculties, and even the frame of the body, are much more affected than when the same people have the same spiritual light and joy afterwards. The reason for this is probably easy to give.

The aforementioned Rev. Lord and Rev. Owen— who, I believe, are known as men of learning and discretion—declared that they found these impressions on people's minds quite different from the idea public opinion had given them. Certainly, no one needs to wonder at, or stumble because of, these spiritual experiences that some people have had.

There have indeed been a few instances of impressions on people's minds that have been somewhat mysterious to me, and I have been at a loss about them. It has been obvious to me, by many things that occurred both then and afterwards, that they indeed had a greater sense of the spiritual excellency of divine things accompanying them. Yet, I have not been able to fully determine for myself whether their ideas have been more than could naturally arise from their spiritual sense of things.

Nevertheless, I have used the utmost caution in such cases; great care has been taken both in public and in private to teach people the difference between what is spiritual and what is merely imaginary. I have often warned people not to put all their hopes on any ideas of outward glory, or any external thing whatsoever, and I have met with no opposition in such instructions. But, some weaker individuals, in giving an account of their experiences, have not so prudently distinguished between the spiritual and imaginary part. Those who have not been inclined toward religion might take advantage of this opportunity to discount the revival.

THE SAME SPIRIT AT WORK

There have also been reports spread around the country that the reason for the increase in religious concerns was a fear that the world was soon coming to an end, which was altogether a false report. Indeed, after religious concerns became so general and extraordinary, as I have related here, the minds of some were filled with speculation about what such a great dispensation of Divine Providence might foretell. Some reports were heard that certain theologians thought the eternal fire was nearing, but such reports were never generally considered as worthy of notice.

The work that has now been performed on souls is evidently the same that took place in my grandfather's days. I had abundant opportunity to know this, since I was in the ministry here two years with him. I have conversed with a considerable number of people whom my grandfather thought to be savingly converted at that time, and I have been particularly acquainted with the experiences of many who were converted under his ministry before that time. None of them, that I know of, doubts in the least that this is the same Spirit and the same work as before. People now have not been subject to any different impressions on their minds than formerly; the work is of the same nature and has not been accompanied by any extraordinary circumstances, excepting those that I have described as somewhat extreme.

God's people who were formerly converted have now partaken of the same shower of divine blessing—in the renewing, strengthening, edifying influences of the Spirit of God—that others have in His converting influences. Indeed, the work here has also been plainly the same as that of other places that have been mentioned. They have all partaken of the same blessing. I have conversed with people in various parts of New England where a religious concern has lately appeared, about their experiences, and I have been informed of the experiences of many others by their own pastors.

CONVERSATIONS CONCERNING THE REVIVAL

It is easily perceived by the foregoing account that it is the practice of the people here to converse freely with one another about their spiritual experiences. Many have been disgusted by this practice. Our people may have, in some respects, gone to extremes in it, but this is a practice that the circumstances of this town and neighboring towns have naturally led them into. Whenever people's minds are focused to a high degree on the same thing, they will naturally make it the subject of conversation when they get together.

And in such conversation, they will grow freer and freer. Restraints will soon vanish, and they will not conceal from one another what they encounter in the spiritual realm. This has been a practice that, in general, has been accompanied by many good effects, and God has greatly blessed it among us. Yet, it must be confessed that there may have been some detrimental consequences of it, which ought to be blamed more on the indiscreet management of it than on the practice itself. So, it really should not be any wonder, among such a multitude, that some fail to exercise much prudence in choosing the desirable time, manner, and occasion for such discourse.

Chapter 8

The Conversion of
Abigail Hutchinson

I n order to give you, the reader, a clearer idea of the nature and manner of the operation of God's Spirit in this revival, I will give an account of two particular instances. The first story, which I will tell in this chapter, is about a young adult, a woman whose name was Abigail Hutchinson.

I mention her especially because she is no longer living, and so I may be able to speak more freely of her than of someone who is alive. Even so, I am disadvantaged by the fact that I cannot give as full and clear a narrative of her experiences as I might of some others. The only account I can give is based upon what has been retained in the memories of her friends, upon what they heard her express in her lifetime.

Abigail was from an intelligent family. Nothing in her education would have caused her to be radical, but rather to the opposite extreme. Her family were not at all ostentatious about their experiences, and so this was far from being her attitude. Even before her conversion, she was thought to have a sober and inoffensive lifestyle; her neighbors and relatives considered her a quiet, reserved person. For a long time she had been prone to sickness, but this tendency had never led her to be foolish or fanciful, nor did it ever cause her any sign of depression over religious matters. She was under the awakening power of the Holy Sprit for scarcely a week before there seemed to be plain evidence of her being savingly converted.

THE FIRST AWAKENING

This young woman was first awakened in the wintertime on a Monday. She had heard her brother say something about the necessity of being earnest in seeking regenerating grace. Abigail had also heard the news of the conversion of the young woman before mentioned, whose conversion so generally affected most of the young people here. This news affected Abigail a great deal. She became a little envious toward the other young woman, whom she thought very unworthy of being set apart from others by such a mercy. Nevertheless, it engaged Abigail in a firm resolution to do her utmost to obtain the same blessing.

When she began to think about what course she should take, she thought she did not have sufficient knowledge of the principles of religion to render her capable of conversion. Upon this consideration, she resolved thoroughly to search the Scriptures. She immediately began at the beginning of the Bible, intending to read it through. She continued thus until that Thursday, and then there was a sudden change. The sense of her own sinfulness, particularly the sinfulness of her nature and the wickedness of her heart, greatly increased in an extraordinary manner. This came upon her, as she expressed it, like a flash of lightning, and it made her very much afraid for her soul. As a result, she stopped reading the Old Testament and the course that she had intended, and she turned to the New Testament to see if she could find some relief there for her distressed soul.

Her great fear, she said, was that she had sinned against God. Her distress grew more and more for three days, until she saw nothing but the blackness of darkness before her, and her very flesh trembled for fear of God's wrath. She was astonished at herself, that she had been so concerned about her body and had gone so often to physicians to heal it, yet had neglected her soul. Her sinfulness appeared very awful to her, especially in three aspects: her original sin; her sin in murmuring at God's providence in the weakness and afflictions she had been under; and her lack of duty to her parents, though others had considered her highly dutiful.

On Saturday, she was very earnestly engaged in reading the Bible and other books, searching for something to relieve her, until her eyes were so tired that she could not make out the letters. While she was thus engaged in reading, prayer, and other religious exercises, she thought of those words of Christ in which He warns us not to be as the heathen, who *think that they shall be heard for their much speaking*" (Matt. 6:7). This, said Abigail, led her to see that she had trusted her own prayers and religious performances, and now she did not know which way to turn or where to seek relief.

While her mind was in this state, she said, her heart seemed to fly to the minister for refuge, hoping that he could give her some relief. With the expression of a person in distress, she went the same day to see her brother, to reason with him as to why he had not told her more about her sinfulness, and to earnestly inquire of him what she should do. She seemed that day to feel in herself an enmity against the Bible, which greatly frightened her. Her sense of her own sinfulness continued to increase from Thursday until the next Monday.

FURTHER CONTEMPLATION

Until that point, it had been her opinion that she was not guilty of Adam's sin, nor was she in any way connected to it, because she was not active in it. However, she now saw that she was guilty of that sin, and completely defiled by it besides. The sin that she brought into the world with her, she knew, was alone sufficient to condemn her.

On the Sabbath day she was so ill that her friends thought it best that she should not go to public worship, though she very much desired to go. However, when she went to bed that night, she resolved that she would go to the minister the next morning, hoping to find some relief there. When she awoke on Monday morning, a little before daylight, she wondered at the easiness and calmness she felt in her mind, which were of a kind she had never felt before.

As Abigail thought of this, such words as these were in her mind: *"The words of the LORD are pure words"* (Ps. 12:6), *"health to* [the soul], *and marrow to* [the] *bones"* (Prov. 3:8). And then these words passed through her thoughts, too: the blood of Christ cleanses from all sin (1 John 1:7). These thoughts were accompanied by a vivid sense of the excellency of Christ and His sufficiency to answer for the sins of the whole world. She then thought of that expression, "It is *'a pleasant thing...for the eyes to behold the sun'* (Eccl. 11:7)," and these words then seemed to her to be very applicable to Jesus Christ.

By these things her mind was led to contemplate Christ in such a way that she was exceedingly filled with joy. That morning she told her brother that she had seen Christ by faith, and that she had thought all along that she did not have enough knowledge to be converted. Yet, she said, God can make it quite easy! All day Monday she felt a constant sweetness in her soul. For three mornings in a row, she had similar experiences of discovering Christ, each time waking a little before daylight. And the experiences grew brighter and brighter every day.

A GROWING LOVE FOR OTHERS

During the last occurrence of this, on Wednesday morning, while enjoying a spiritual experience of Christ's glory and fullness, Abigail's soul was filled with distress for people who did not know Christ. She began to consider what a miserable condition they were in. She immediately felt a strong inclination to go forth and warn sinners. The next day she asked her brother to assist her in going from house to house, but he restrained her by telling her of the unsuitableness of such a method.

That day, Abigail told one of her sisters that she loved all mankind, especially the people of God. Her sister asked her why she loved all mankind. She replied, "Because God has made them." After this, three people who had recently been converted happened to come into the shop where she was at work. When she saw them, as they stepped in one after another, she was so moved with love for them that it overcame her, and she almost fainted. When they began to talk of the things of religion, it was more than she could bear, so they had to cease talking about it for the time. Abigail was frequently overcome with the flow of affection for those whom she thought godly, especially when she was involved in conversation with them, and sometimes only at the sight of them.

DISCOVERIES OF THE ATTRIBUTES OF GOD

Abigal had many extraordinary discoveries of the glory of God and Christ. Sometimes she would discover God in some particular attribute, and sometimes in many. She once testified that, when wisdom, justice, goodness, and truth passed through her mind, her soul was filled with a sense of the glory of each of these divine attributes, but especially the last. Truth, she said, sunk the deepest! Therefore, as these things passed through her, this was repeated: "Truth, truth!" Her mind was so swallowed up with a sense of the glory of God's truth and other perfections that she said it seemed as though her life was fading away, and that God could easily take away her life by revealing Himself to her.

Soon after this, she went to a private religious meeting, and her mind was full of a sense of the glory of God the entire time. When the meeting had ended, some asked her about what she had experienced, and she began to give an account of it. But, as she was relating the experience, a sense of the same things revived in her soul, her strength failed, and they were obliged to take her and lay her upon the bed. Afterwards she was greatly affected and rejoiced with these words: *"Worthy is the Lamb that was slain"* (Rev. 5:12).

For several days in a row, Abigail had a sweet sense of the excellency and loveliness of Christ in His meekness. This caused her to continually repeat these words, which were very sweet to her: *"meek and lowly in heart"* (Matt. 11:29), *"meek and lowly in heart."* She once told one of her sisters that she had continued whole days and whole nights in a constant ravishing view of the glory of God and Christ, having enjoyed as much as her life could bear. Once, as her brother was speaking of the dying love of Christ, she told him that she had such a sense of it that the mere mentioning of it was ready to overcome her.

Abigail once told me of a time when she thought she saw as much of God and had as much joy and pleasure as was possible in this life. And yet, afterwards, God revealed Himself far more abundantly to her. She saw the same things as before, yet more clearly and in a far more excellent and delightful manner, and she was filled with a more exceptional sweetness. Likewise, she gave me such an account of the sense she once had from day to day of the glory of Christ and of God in His various attributes, that it seemed to me she dwelt for days on end in a kind of blissful vision of God. In fact, she seemed to have the sort of immediate contact with Him that a child has with a father.

A HUMBLE HEART

At the same time, Abigail was far from having any high thoughts of herself and of her own sufficiency. Rather, she was like a little child who expresses a great desire to be instructed. She told me that she longed very often to come to me for instruction and wanted to live at my house, so that I might tell her what was her duty as a believer.

For Abigail, the glory of God appeared in the trees, the growth of the fields, and other works of His hands. She told her sister who lived near the center of town that she once thought it a pleasant thing to live in the middle of town, but now she found it much more pleasant to sit and see the wind blowing the trees and to behold in the country what God has made. Sometimes the powerful breathings of the Spirit of God would move on her soul while she was reading the Scripture, and she would express her sense of the certain truth and divinity of the Word of God. Sometimes she would have such a pleasant smile on her face that once, when her sister took notice of it and asked why she smiled, she replied, "I am entirely filled with a sweet feeling within."

Abigail often expressed how good and sweet it was to lie low before God, and the lower the better! She also said that it was pleasant to think of lying in the dust all the days of her life, mourning for sin. Her general demeanor served to manifest a great sense of her own lowliness and dependence. Abigail often expressed a great compassion and pitiful love toward those who were without Christ. This was sometimes so strong that, as she passed by such people in the streets, or those whom she feared were such, she would be overcome by the sight of them. She once said that she longed to have the whole world saved. She wanted to pull them all to herself, for she could not bear to have one lost.

Abigail longed to die, so that she might sooner be with Christ. This desire increased until she thought she could no longer be patient and wait until God's time. Yet, once, when she felt those longings, she thought within herself, "If I long to die, why do I go to physicians?" After this, she concluded that her longings for death were not well regulated. So she often asked herself which she should choose, whether to live or to die, to be sick or to be well. She found she could not tell what she wanted, until at last she found herself saying these words: "I am quite willing to live and quite willing to die, quite willing to be sick and quite willing to be well, and quite willing for anything that God will bring upon me!"

After this, she claimed she felt perfectly at ease, in full submission to the will of God. She then lamented that she had been so eager for death, for such eagerness was evidence that she was not as resigned to God's will as she ought to be. From that point until her death, she seemed to continue in this state of a resigned will.

A RESIGNED WILL

But then, her illness grew worse. Once, after she had spent the greater part of the night in extreme pain, she awoke out of a little sleep with these words in her heart and mouth: "I am willing to suffer for

Christ's sake. I am willing to spend and be spent for Christ's sake. I am willing to spend my life, even my very life, for Christ's sake!" And though she had an extraordinary resignation with respect to life or death, the thoughts of dying were very sweet to her.

At a time when Abigail's brother was reading in the book of Job about worms feeding on the dead body (Job 19:26), a pleasant smile came over her face. When she was asked about it, she said, "It is sweet to think of myself being in such circumstances." At another time, when her brother mentioned that the illness she suffered under might be the cause of her death, it filled her with joy that almost overcame her. And when she met a company of mourners following a corpse to the grave, she said it was sweet to think that they would in a little time follow her in a similar manner.

Her illness, in the latter part of it, was mostly in her throat. An inward swelling filled up her esophagus so that she could swallow nothing but what was perfectly liquid. Even then, she could swallow very little of that without a great struggle. Everything she took in through her mouth came back out through her nostrils, until at last she could swallow nothing at all. She had such a raging appetite for food that she told her sister, when talking with her about her circumstances, that even the worst bit of food would be sweet to her. Yet, when she saw that she could not swallow it, she seemed to be as perfectly contented without it as if she had no appetite.

Others were greatly moved to see what she underwent and were filled with admiration for her patience. Once, when she was striving in vain to get down a little liquid and was very much exhausted by the effort, she looked at her sister with a smile, saying, "O sister, this is for my good!" At another time, when her sister was speaking of what she underwent, Abigail told her that she lived a heaven upon earth despite all that she had undergone. She used to say to her sister sometimes, under her extreme sufferings, "It is good to be so!" Her sister once asked her why she said so. "Why," said Abigail, "because God would have it so! It is best that things should be as God would have them. Therefore, it looks best to me."

Once, as they were leading her from the bed to the door, she seemed overcome by the sight of things abroad, as they showed forth the glory of the Being who had made them. As she lay on her deathbed, she often said, "God is my Friend!" And once, looking at her sister with a smile, she said, "O sister, how good it is! How sweet and comfortable it is to consider and think of heavenly things!" This persuaded her sister to meditate often on these things.

On her deathbed, Abigail expressed a great longing that people in a natural state might be converted and that the godly might see and know more of God. When those in a Christless state came to see her, she was greatly moved with compassionate affection for them. One girl in particular seemed to be in great distress about the state of her soul and had come to see Abigail from time to time. Abigail, however, desired her sister to persuade this visitor not to come anymore, because the sight of this person caused a wave of compassion to overcome Abigail's already weak body.

The same week that Abigail died, when the condition of her body seemed quite distressing, some of her neighbors came to see her and asked if she was willing to die. She replied that she was quite willing either to live or die; she was willing to be in pain; she was willing to be ill forever, if that was the will of God. She willed what God willed. They asked her if she was willing to die that night. She answered, "Yes, if it is God's will." And she seemed to speak with a perfect composure of spirit and with such a cheerful and pleasant countenance that it filled them with admiration.

NO FEAR OF DEATH

She was very weak for a considerable time before she died, having wasted away with famine and thirst so that her flesh seemed to be dried upon her bones. Therefore, she could say very little, and she had to communicate with a sort of sign language. She said she had enough to say that all her time could be spent talking, if she had the strength. A few days before her death, some asked her if she was afraid of death. She answered that she did not have even the least degree of fear of death. They asked her why she would be so confident. She answered, "If I were to say otherwise, I would be speaking contrary to what I know. There is, indeed, an entry that looks somewhat dark, but on the other side there is such a bright shining light that I cannot be afraid!"

Not long before she died, she said that the thought of grappling with death used to frighten her. However, she said, "God has showed me that He can make it easy, even in great pain." Several days before she died, she could scarcely say anything but just yes or no to questions that were asked her, for she seemed to be dying for three days in a row. Nevertheless, she seemed to continue to the end in an admirably sweet composure of soul without any interruption, and she died as a person who went to sleep, without any struggling, around noon on Friday, June 27, 1735.

Although her body had lacked strength for quite a while, and although she had experienced much pain, she died chiefly from starvation. Her bodily weakness was doubtless the major reason why she was so often overcome and ready to sink down under feelings of God's grace. The truth was that she had more grace and greater discoveries of God and Christ than her human body could handle. She wanted to be where strong grace could have more liberty with her soul, where she could be without the encumbrance of a weak body. She longed to be in heaven, and doubtless she is there now.

The case of Abigail Hutchinson was considered a very eminent instance of Christian experience, but this is a very broken and imperfect account of her life. Abigail's eminency would be far more obvious here if she were still alive to tell me of her experiences. I once read this account to some of her pious neighbors who were acquainted with her, and they said that the picture I give here falls far short of the life she lived. Particularly, my words fail to fully represent her humility and the admirable lowliness of heart that appeared in her at all times. Nonetheless, blessed be God that there are many living instances in which things no less extraordinary have occurred.

Chapter 9

The Conversion of Phebe Bartlet

I now proceed to the other instance, that of the four-year-old child whom I mentioned in chapter three. Her name is Phebe Bartlet. I will give the account of Phebe's conversion as I received it from her parents, whose truthfulness is not doubted by anyone who knows them.

She was born in March 1731. Around the end of April or the beginning of May 1735, she was greatly affected by the talk of her brother, who had been converted a little before that time. He talked seriously to her about the great things of religion. Her parents did not know of it at that time, and they were not likely to direct the sort of counsel to her that they gave to their other children, especially when she was so young and, as they supposed, not capable of understanding. But, after her brother had talked to her, they observed Phebe very earnestly listen to the advice they gave to the other children.

Very often, she was seen going several times a day to a quiet closet, and it was concluded that she did so for secret prayer. She grew more and more engaged in religion and went more frequently to this closet, until at last she was likely to visit it five or six times a day. She was so involved in it that nothing would at any time divert her from her intended exercises. Her mother often watched her when something occurred that would be likely to divert her. But the young girl never put religion out of her thoughts or gave in to her more natural inclinations. Phebe's mother mentioned some very remarkable instances of this.

A STRUGGLE TO FIND GOD

Once, of her own accord, Phebe spoke of her failure to find God. But, on the last day of July, about the middle of the day, the child was heard speaking aloud in the closet. This was unusual and had never been observed before. Her voice seemed to be the voice of one who is greatly engaged in persistent prayer, yet her mother could distinctly hear only these words, spoken in a childish manner but with extraordinary earnestness and out of distress of soul: "Blessed Lord, give me salvation! Pardon all my sins!"

When Phebe had finished praying, she came out of the closet, sat down by her mother, and cried out loud. Mrs. Bartlet very earnestly asked her several times what the matter was, before Phebe could give any answer. She continued crying, and her body shook like one in anguish of spirit. Her mother then asked her if she was afraid that God would not give her salvation. She then answered, "Yes, I am afraid I will go to hell!" Mrs. Bartlet then attempted to quiet her and told her she would not have her cry, that she must be a good girl and pray every day, and that she hoped God would give her salvation. But this did not quiet her at all. She continued earnestly crying and carrying on for some time, until she suddenly ceased crying and began to smile. She said, "Mother, the kingdom of heaven is come to me!"

Mrs. Bartlet was surprised at the sudden change in Phebe, and at the words the girl used. In fact, she did not know what to make of it, so at first she said nothing to her. The child then spoke again and said, "Another has come to me, and another, and now there are three." When her mother asked what she meant, she answered, "One is, *'Thy will be done'* (Matt. 6:10), and there is another, 'Enjoy Him forever.' So, in other words, when Phebe said, "Three have come to me," she meant three passages of her catechism that came to her mind.

Salvation Brings Joy

After Phebe had said this, she retired again into her closet. Mrs. Bartlet, meanwhile, went to see Phebe's brother. When she came back, the child, having already emerged from the closet, met her mother with these cheerful words: "I can find God now!" This was in reference to what she had complained of earlier, that she could not find God. Then the child spoke again and said, "I love God!" Her mother asked her how much she loved God, whether she loved God better than her father and mother. She said, "Yes." Then Mrs. Bartlet asked her whether she loved God better than her little sister Rachel. She answered, "Yes, better than anything!"

Then Phebe's older sister, referring to the statement that she could find God now, asked her, "Where can you find God?" She answered, "In heaven." So the sister asked, "Have you been in heaven?" "No," said the child. Thus, when she said, "I can find God now," it seems that the thing she called God was not something that can be seen with the natural eyes. Her mother asked her whether she was afraid of going to hell, and if that had made her cry. She answered, "Yes, I was, but now I will not be afraid anymore." Then Mrs. Bartlet asked her if she thought that God had given her salvation. Phebe answered, "Yes." "When?" asked her mother. "Today."

That afternoon, Phebe was very cheerful and joyful. One of the neighbors asked her how she felt. She answered, "I feel better than I did." The neighbor asked her, "What makes you feel better?" She answered, "God does." That evening, as she lay in bed, she called one of her little cousins to her, who was present in the room, as if she had something to say to him. When he came, she told him that heaven was better than earth. The next day, her mother asked her, "Why has God put you here?" She answered, "To serve Him." And she added, "Everybody should serve God and get an interest in Christ."

A Great Burden for Others' Salvation

The same day, when the older children came home from school, they seemed very much affected by the extraordinary change that had occurred in Phebe. In fact, her mother happily used Phebe's example to advise her sister Abigail to use her time to prepare for another world. This caused Phebe to burst out in tears and cry out, using her sister's nickname, "Poor Nabby!" Her mother told her she would not have to cry; she hoped that God would give Nabby salvation. But that did not quiet her, and she continued earnestly crying for some time. When Phebe had ceased crying for the most part, her sister Eunice was near her, and she burst out again and cried, "Poor Eunice!" and cried exceedingly. When she had almost finished, she went into another room and saw her sister Naomi. Again she burst out crying, "Poor Amy!"

Of course, her mother was greatly thrown off by such behavior in a child and did not know what to say to her. One of the neighbors came in a little while later and asked Phebe what she had cried for. At first she seemed unwilling to tell the reason. Then her mother told her she could tell that person, so she then admitted that she had cried because she was afraid her sisters would go to hell.

Strong Emotions

At night, a certain minister was at the house, and he talked about religious things with her. After he was gone, she sat, leaning on the table, with tears running from her eyes. When she was asked what made her cry, she said, "I was thinking about God." During most of the next day, Saturday, she seemed to be in a very emotional state of mind. She had four long periods of crying and seemed to try the whole day to hold back or hide her tears. She was very reluctant to talk about why she was crying. On Sunday, she was asked whether she believed in God. She answered, "Yes." And when she was told that Christ was the Son of God, she answered by saying, "I know it."

LASTING CHANGES

Since that time, there has been a very remarkable and abiding change in the young child. She has been very disciplined in keeping the Sabbath. Indeed, she seems to long for the Sabbath day before it comes, and she will often inquire during the week how long it is until Sunday. She then insists on counting the days in between, before she will be contented. She seems to love God's house and is very eager to go there. Her mother once asked her why she was so eager to go. Was it to see other people? She said, "No, it is to hear Mr. Edwards preach."

When she is in the place of worship, she is very far from spending her time there as children of her age usually do. Instead, she seems to have an attention span that is very extraordinary for such a child. She also seems very desirous of all opportunities to go to private religious meetings. She is very still and attentive at home during prayer and becomes emotional in times of family prayer.

Phebe also seems to delight in hearing religious conversation. Once, when some strangers and I were at her home and talked to her about religion, she seemed more than ordinarily attentive. When we were gone, she looked out very wistfully after us and said, "I wish they would come again!" Her mother asked her, "Why?" so she said, "I love to hear them talk."

A GREATER SENSE OF SIN

Phebe seems to be full of the fear of God, with an extraordinary dread of sinning against Him. Concerning this, her mother mentioned the following remarkable instance. Sometime in August of last year, she went with some older children to get some plums in a neighbor's yard, unaware of any harm in what she did. But, when she brought some of the plums into the house, her mother mildly scolded her and told her that she must not pick plums without permission, because it was a sin to steal them. God had commanded her not to steal. The child seemed greatly surprised and burst out in tears, and she cried out, "I won't have these plums!" She then turned to her sister Eunice and very earnestly said to her, "Why did you ask me to go to that plum tree? I would not have gone if you had not asked me."

The other children did not seem to be concerned about it, but there was no pacifying Phebe. Her mother told her she could ask permission from the neighbor, and then it would not be a sin for her to eat them. One of the children was sent out to do just that. When the sibling returned, Mrs. Bartlet told Phebe that the owner had given permission and that now she could eat the plums, for it would not be stealing.

This quieted her for a little while, but soon enough she broke out again into a fit of tears. Her mother asked her, "What makes you cry again? You have permission to eat the plums. What is troubling you now?" Mrs. Bartlet asked her several times very earnestly before Phebe gave any answer. At last she said, "It was because, because it was a sin." She continued crying for a considerable time and said she would not go again if Eunice asked her a hundred times. After that, she had an aversion to plums for a long time, for they reminded her of her former sin.

DELIGHT IN SCRIPTURE

She sometimes appears greatly affected by and delighted with verses of Scripture that come to her mind. Particularly around the beginning of November of last year, this verse would often emerge in her thoughts:

> *Behold, I stand at the door, and knock: if any man hear my voice, and open the door, I will come in to him, and will sup with him, and he with me.* *(Rev. 3:20)*

At the time, Phebe spoke of this verse to her family with great joy, a smiling face, and elevation of voice. After she did so, she went into another room where her mother overheard her talking very earnestly to the other children about it. Mrs. Bartlet heard her say to them, three or four times over, with great joy and admiration, "It means that we may dine with God!"

OTHER MANIFESTATIONS OF SALVATION

Sometime in the middle of winter, very late in the night, when all were in bed, her mother heard the sound of weeping and perceived that Phebe was awake. She called to Phebe and asked her what was the matter. She answered with such a low voice that her mother could not hear what she said. Thinking that the crying might have been caused by some spiritual emotion, Mrs. Bartlet said no more to her. Instead, she perceived that Phebe lay awake and continued in the same manner for a considerable time. The next morning she asked Phebe if she had cried during the night. The child answered, "Yes, I did cry a little, for I was thinking about God and Christ, and they loved me." Her mother asked her if thinking about God and Christ loving her made her cry. She answered, "Yes, it does sometimes."

Phebe has often manifested a great concern for the good of others' souls; many times she has affectionately counseled the other children. Once, around the end of September 1735, she and some of the other children were in a room by themselves, husking corn. After a while, Phebe came out and sat by the fire. Her mother noticed that she had an unusually serious and pensive look on her face, but at last she broke her silence and said, "I have been talking to Nabby and Eunice." Her mother asked her what she had said to them. "Well," said Phebe, "I told them they must pray and prepare to die; that they have but a little while to live in this world, and they must be always ready." When Abigail came out of the room, her mother asked her if Phebe had said that to them. "Yes," said Abigail, "she said that and a great deal more."

At other times, Phebe took opportunities to talk to the other children about the great concern of their souls, so much that it affected them. She was once very persistent in asking her mother to pray with her sister Naomi. Mrs. Bartlet tried to put her off, but Phebe pulled her by the sleeve and seemed as if she would not be refused. At last her mother told her that Amy must go and pray by herself. "But," said Phebe, "she will not go," and she persisted to earnestly beg her mother to go with her.

This young child has discovered an uncommon degree of the spirit of charity. This is shown particularly by the following story. A poor man who lives in the woods recently lost the cow that his family much depended on. While he was visiting the Bartlets, he was relating his misfortune and telling of the difficulties it had brought them. Phebe took much notice of the man's situation, and it greatly moved her to compassion.

After she had attentively heard him for a while, she went to her father, who was in the shop, and entreated him to give that man a cow. She told him, "That poor man has no cow! The hunters, or something else, killed his cow!" and she entreated him to give him one of theirs. Her father told her that they could not spare one. Then she entreated him to let the man and his family come and live at his house. By this she manifested her compassion for the poor.

She has also manifested great love to her minister, particularly when I returned last fall from my long journey for my health. When she heard that I had returned, she appeared very joyful at the news and told the other children about it with an elevated voice. It was as if these were the most joyful tidings, and she repeated them over and over. "Mr. Edwards has come home! Mr. Edwards has come home!"

Phebe still continues to be diligent in secret prayer, as far as can be observed, for she seems to have no desire that others should observe her when she goes to her prayer closet, being a child of a reserved temper. Every night before she goes to bed, she says her catechism and will not miss a day for anything. She only forgot it once, and in that case, after she was in bed, she thought of it and cried out in tears, "I haven't said my catechism!" She would not go to sleep until her mother asked her the catechism as she lay in bed.

Sometimes when Phebe is asked whether she thinks she is prepared for death, she seems to have no doubt and says, "Yes," without hesitation. Truly, this young child has experienced the converting power of the Holy Spirit of God.

Chapter 10

The Gradual Withdrawing
of the Holy Spirit

I n the earlier part of this great work of God among us, until it reached its peak, we seemed to be wonderfully smiled upon and blessed in all respects. Satan seemed to be unusually restrained; people who had been stricken with depression seemed to be awakened out of it, and those who had been entangled by extraordinary temptations seemed wonderfully freed. Not only that, but it was also the most remarkable time of health that I ever knew since I have been in the town of Northampton. We ordinarily have several petitions raised to God every Sunday for sick people, but during the revival we did not have even one for many Sundays on end. But, after the revival, it seemed to be otherwise.

EVIDENCE OF THE DEVIL AT WORK AGAIN

When this work of God appeared to be at its greatest height, a poor weak man who lives in the town, who was in great spiritual trouble, experienced violent temptations to cut his own throat. In fact, he attempted to kill himself in this manner but did not succeed. After this, he was for a long time exceedingly overwhelmed by depression, but now he has been very greatly delivered by the light of God's countenance lifted upon him. He has expressed a great sense of his sin in yielding so far to such a temptation, and there is much evidence in him that he has been a recipient of God's saving mercy.

In the latter part of May 1736, it began to be very obvious that the Spirit of God was gradually withdrawing from us, for after this time Satan seemed to be more on the loose, raging in a dreadful manner. The first instance in which this appeared was a different person putting an end to his own life by cutting his throat. He was a gentleman of more than common understanding, of strict morals, disciplined in his behavior, and a useful and honorable person in the town. Yet, he came from a family that has been exceedingly prone to depression; his mother suffered from it so much that she died.

From the beginning of this extraordinary time of revival, this man had been highly concerned about the state of his soul, and there were some things in his experience that appeared very hopeful. Nevertheless, he did not dare to entertain any hope concerning his own good estate. Toward the latter part of his life, he grew very discouraged, and depression raged again within him until he was wholly overpowered by it.

The depression was so great that he lost the capacity to receive advice or to be reasoned with. Indeed, the Devil took advantage of him and drove him into despairing thoughts. He was kept awake at night, dwelling in terror, so that he had scarcely any sleep at all for many days at a time. At last people began to notice that he was hardly capable of managing his ordinary business, and he was judged to have been delirious by the coroner's examination.

The news of this man extraordinarily affected the minds of people here and struck them with astonishment. After this, multitudes in this and other towns seemed to be tempted very much to do as this person had done. Even those who seemed to have no depression at all—some pious individuals who had no special darkness or doubts about the goodness of their state, nor were undergoing any special trouble or concern in their minds about anything spiritual or temporal—felt as if somebody had said to them, "Cut your throat. Now is a good opportunity. Now! Now!" Thus, they were obliged to fight with all their might to resist it, and yet there was no reason why they should have had to fight it in the first place.

DELUSIONAL THOUGHTS ARISE

About the same time, there were two remarkable instances of individuals who were led astray by strange, enthusiastic delusions. One was in Suffield, and the other in South Hadley. The man in South Hadley has caused the most disturbance among the people of this region, so I mention his case in more detail. He had been deluded into thinking himself divinely instructed to direct a poor man, who was in depressing and despairing circumstances, to say certain words in prayer to God for his relief. The words of the prayer are found in Psalm 116:4: *"O LORD, I beseech thee, deliver my soul."*

The man is regarded as a pious man, and since this error of his, I have become better acquainted with him. I believe no one who has such acquaintance with him would question his piety. He told me the particular details of how he was deluded, and, in short, how he had been carried away by the extraordinary work that had taken place in this part of the country. This led him to think that this revival was the beginning of the glorious times of the church spoken of in Scripture.

He had read that some theologians thought the same thing, and that many people in these times would be endued with extraordinary gifts of the Holy Spirit. He had embraced this idea for himself, although he did not know for certain that anyone besides ministers would have such gifts. However, since then, he regrets the dishonor he has done to God and the wound he has given religion by his actions, and he has lain low before God and man for it.

A GENERAL DECLINE OF RELIGIOUS CONVERSIONS

Although the remarkable instance of Phebe Bartlet did occur after the highest point of the revival, the instances of conversion were rare in Northampton after this peak in comparison with what they had been before. Not long after this time, the Spirit of God very obviously was withdrawing from all parts of the region, though we have heard of the work going on in some parts of Connecticut, where it continues to be carried on even to this day. Nevertheless, religion remained the main subject of conversation here in Northampton and in some other places for several months after. There were even some periods of time in which God's work seemed to revive, and we were ready to hope that all was going to be renewed again. Yet, in general, there was a gradual decline of that overall, engaged, lively spirit in religion, which had been seen during the revival.

Several things have happened since, which have diverted people's minds and turned their conversation more to other affairs. In particular, people were more inclined to concern themselves with the treaty with the Indians, the Springfield controversy, or the building of a new meetinghouse. Many other events have had a similar effect.

THE PEOPLE REMAIN CHANGED

Even so, those who have been converted in this revival generally seem to have had an abiding change take place in them. I have been particularly acquainted with many of them since, and they generally appear to be people who have a new sense of things: new understandings and views of God, the divine attributes of Jesus Christ, and the great things of the Gospel. They have a new sense of the Gospel truth, and they show this in a new manner. They show it in many different ways as time goes on, for they cannot revive the same sense of such things whenever they please.

Their hearts are often touched and sometimes filled with new sweetnesses and delights. There seems to be an inward ardor and burning of heart, which they never experienced before. Sometimes, perhaps, this is occasioned only by the mention of Christ's name. There are new appetites and a new kind of desire in the heart and *"groanings which cannot be uttered"* (Rom. 8:26). There is a new kind of inward labor and struggle of soul toward heaven and holiness.

Some who used to be very rough in their disposition and manners seemed to be remarkably softened and sweetened. Others have been exceedingly filled and overwhelmed with light, love, and comfort, long after the work of God had ceased to be so remarkably carried on in a general way. And some, since that time, have had much greater experiences of this nature than they had before.

There is still a great deal of religious conversation continued in the town among both young and old. A religious disposition also appears to be maintained among our people, as is evidenced by their holding frequent private religious meetings. All kinds of people are generally worshipping God at such meetings on Sunday evenings and in the evenings after our public lectures. Many children in the town still keep up such meetings among themselves. I know of no young person in the town who has returned to former ways of looseness and extravagance in any respect. Instead, we remain a reformed people, and God has evidently made us a new people.

I cannot say that there has been no case of someone conducting himself unworthily. Nor am I so vain as to imagine that we have not been mistaken in our good opinion concerning some people. Some among us pass for sheep yet are indeed wolves in sheep's clothing. These, at some time or another, will probably reveal themselves by their fruits. (See Matthew 7:15–16.) We are not entirely pure; rather, we have great cause to be humbled and ashamed that we are so impure. Nor are we wholly religious; those who watch for us to stumble may see many things in us by which they may reproach us and our religion. (See Jeremiah 20:10.)

But, in general, there has been a great and marvelous work of conversion and sanctification among the people here. They have paid all due respect to those who have been blessed by God as the instruments of the work. Both young and old have shown a readiness to listen not only to my counsels, but also to my reproofs, from the pulpit.

REPORTS OF GOD'S WORK

People in many parts of the country have not received the most favorable reports of this revival, and to this day they retain a jealousy concerning it and a prejudice against it. I have reason to think that the lowliness and weakness of the instrument whom God has used in this town has prejudiced many against it. Yet it does not appear strange to me that it should be so.

The fact that God would use a weak instrument like myself is analogous to other circumstances of the work of God. God has ordered the work in such as way as to show that it is His own particular and immediate work. Through all the circumstances surrounding the revival, God has intended to secure the glory of it wholly to His almighty power and sovereign grace. Whatever the means have been to carry on this work, and though we are so unworthy, yet it has pleased God to work in such a way. We are evidently a people blessed by God! For here, in this corner of the world, God dwells and manifests His glory.

PRAY FOR THE PEOPLE OF GOD

I have given a long and detailed account of this remarkable revival; yet, considering how manifold God's works have been among us, it is but a very brief one. It is perhaps longer than my readers would have liked, but I thought that the extraordinary nature of the revival made it necessary to be particular. Besides, many false reports have gone along with the revival and have doubtless misrepresented God's power throughout the work.

I ask you to use this account in a way that brings the most glory to God and that furthers the interest of religion. Pray at the throne of grace that God would not forsake His people, but that He would enable us to bring forth fruit according to our profession of faith and our mercies. Pray that our light may shine before men in such a way that, when others see our good works, they may glorify our Father who is in heaven (Matt. 5:16).

I humbly request your prayers for every region in which God's Holy Spirit has seemed to withdraw. These are distressing circumstances. The Springfield quarrel, above all else, has tended to put a stop to the glorious work here in Northampton, to turn this country against it, and to hinder the furthering of God's work. I also ask your prayers for all the residents of these towns. I hope that I have shown you, through this account, God's hand in this wonderful work, the Great Awakening.